Trauma in 20th Century Multicultural American Poetry

READING TRAUMA AND MEMORY

Series Editors: Aimee Pozorski, Central Connecticut State University
and Nicholas Ealy, University of Hartford

Reading Trauma and Memory offers global perspectives on representations of trauma and memory while examining the tensions, limitations, and responsibilities that accompany the status of the witness. This series attempts to bridge the gap between trauma studies and new directions in the fields of memory studies, popular culture, and race theory and seeks submissions that closely read literature and culture for representations of traumatic wounding, the limits of memory, and the ethical duty to depict historical trauma and its effects.

Given its breadth, this series will appeal to scholars in a number of interdisciplinary fields; given the specific angle of trauma and memory, it will capture those who see ethics and responsibility as key factors in their scholarship. Such areas include: Holocaust studies; war trauma and PTSD; illness and disability; the trauma of migration and immigration; memory studies; race studies; gender and sexuality studies (which has recently had a resurgence with the #MeToo movement); studies in popular culture that take up television and films about witness; and the study of social and historical movements.

We are seeking projects that question how to honor the past through close readings of literature focused on trauma and memory—which would necessarily take on international perspectives. Examples include a consideration of literature, justice, and Rwanda through a postcolonial and trauma lens; recent thinking on the phenomenon of "American Crime Story" and the resurgence of interest in the OJ Simpson trial that parallels the narrative of the Black Lives Matter movement; readings of the attempts of popular culture to address issues of historical injustice as exemplified by *12 Years a Slave* and HBO's *Westworld*.

Recent Titles in This Series

Occupying Memory: Rhetoric, Trauma, Mourning
By Trevor Hoag

Literary and Visual Representations of HIV/AIDS: Forty Years Later
By Aimee Pozorski, Jennifer Lavoie, and Christine Cynn

Ethics of Witness in Global Testimonial Narratives: Responding to the Pain of Others
By Kimberly Nance

Trauma in 20th Century Multicultural American Poetry: Unmuted Verse
By Jamie D. Barker

Trauma in 20th Century Multicultural American Poetry

Unmuted Verse

Jamie D. Barker

LEXINGTON BOOKS
Lanham • Boulder • New York • London

Published by Lexington Books
An imprint of The Rowman & Littlefield Publishing Group, Inc.
4501 Forbes Boulevard, Suite 200, Lanham, Maryland 20706
www.rowman.com

6 Tinworth Street, London SE11 5AL, United Kingdom

Copyright © 2020 by The Rowman and Littlefield Publishing Group, Inc.

All rights reserved. No part of this book may be reproduced in any form or by any electronic or mechanical means, including information storage and retrieval systems, without written permission from the publisher, except by a reviewer who may quote passages in a review.

British Library Cataloguing in Publication Information Available

Library of Congress Cataloging-in-Publication Data

Library of Congress Control Number:2019954143
ISBN 978-1-4985-9269-7 (cloth)
ISBN 978-1-4985-9271-0 (paper)
ISBN 978-1-4985-9270-3 (electronic)

Contents

Foreword	vii
Acknowledgments	xi
Chapter One	1
Chapter Two	31
Chapter Three	69
Chapter Four	103
Afterword	143
Bibliography	145
Index	151
About the Author	155

Foreword

During my senior year of high school, I decided to transfer to a larger school in hopes that a Division I university would offer me a scholarship to play football. That scholarship never came, but it did result in the interest in a vastly different type of scholarship. I grew up and lived in a very, very white community. The school that I transferred to was in a town that was home to only one African American family. The other school was not nearly so diverse.

One benefit that I had by playing football was that I was able to meet quite a few people before the school year officially started. That is where I met Alex. Alex isn't his real name, but I have settled on that name. Alex was the only African American male in the high school. He was also an incoming freshman and a mediocre athlete. Alex was accepted by everyone on the team and, as I would come to learn later, everyone in the school.

The first day of school came and another black face appeared in the crowded hallway. I didn't know him. I didn't really know anyone. I didn't even know the teachers. What I didn't realize until later was that no one knew him. He had transferred in from another school after getting in some trouble, but his short stint at this school was nothing like The Fresh Prince of Bel-Air.

I remember hearing ethnic slurs being flung at him by the end of the day. I thought it was odd. Alex was black. These same angry faces seemed to adore Alex, but this young man was obviously not welcome. I did not know how to respond. I was confused and frightened. I couldn't imagine how he felt.

The next day, I noticed that several of the pickup trucks the boys brought to school had started flying Confederate flags. There was no mistake what this implied; we were in a northern state, and this was not about "heritage" or "pride."

On the third day, someone had broken into his locker and hung a noose. I don't know who it was. I also did not know how to respond to all of this. I wanted it to stop. I wanted them to understand that he was no different than Alex, whom they like, except that he was new. In that regard, he wasn't any different than me, except he was black. I tried to talk to the people whom I played ball with, but they either were too young and cowards like me, or they were actually some of the ones doing these things.

I wanted to help him, and on the fourth day, I got my chance.

He came up to me in the hallway. He had been beaten the night before. His left eye was swollen shut, his lip was split, his jaw was wired shut, and the gauze in his mouth still held blood. He asked me where Mrs. Spencer's classroom was. I paused, looked at him and said, "I don't know."

The truth is that I didn't know. I know I would have told him if I did, but I was just a new as he was, and I wasn't even sure of the names of all my teachers yet. After all, it was only the fourth day of class.

After I told him that I didn't know, he looked at me, and the expression on his face, and the look in his eye, said that I was just another one. I was another person who wouldn't help him. I was another white face who sneered and spit and called him slurs. I was one of those who flew that hateful flag. I was one who planted the noose in his locker. I had one of the fists that beat his face. I was no different than any other person he had met.

He walked away shaking his head, but I stood there in silence.

A change occurred in me at that moment. I knew what I wanted to fight against. I knew the hate that I saw, and the reaction that he had was something I never wanted to see again. I knew that that hate was what I wanted to spend my life fighting against.

He never returned after that day.

I don't know if he went home or ran away or died. I don't know his name, who he was, or if he was able to rise above.

The trauma he incurred was both firsthand and the result of historical trauma that still infects this nation today. In graduate school I worked as an editorial assistant to the psychological journal *Anxiety, Stress, and Coping*. Reading those articles gave me new insight into psychology and forced themselves into my thoughts as I continued to study minority literature. Eventually, I was introduced to literary trauma theory, and I knew my calling.

Not long after, I worked at a college in a very impoverished part of Georgia. Our students were mainly from the area. The population of the area and the population of the school were mainly African American. Knowing this, and keeping the young man spoken of earlier in my heart, I was able to create African American literature classes to be taught, for the first time, at the college. The classes filled very quickly, and the students thirsted for the knowledge about African American literature and the history that went along with it. They were able to grow as young people by learning and knowing that some of the writers we read, and the fictions they produced, had encountered some of the same hate, racism, bigotry, and poverty that they had (and still were). Many found solace in this idea that they were not alone nor was their generation. The same can be said for the traumatic experiences some faced. Several former servicemen and -women spoke of how much the poetry of Yusef Komunyakaa spoke to them, even though the wars and times were different.

In 2017, two of my students were shot and killed in separate events. I was taken aback by these events. Many of my students had missed class because they had been incarcerated or had to "bail out" a family member. I still remember being handed the strange documentation, which comes from being locked in jail, that was given to me by several students. Some of my students were active or former gang members. Some were homeless. Some were dealing with PTSD, and others were working three or four jobs to get by, all while taking classes. One student confessed, shortly after the senseless murder of Trayvon Martin, that he was his cousin. For those who need my help, I sent them to the people on campus who may be able to help them. I know that there is only so much that a professor can do and usually it feels like it is nowhere near enough.

But those two young, black men killed in senseless violence and the one who was beaten and bloodied in high school resonate with me every day.

This tome is dedicated to them and the millions like them, who have suffered at the hands of bigots and who were let down by people like me.

This will not atone for the wrongdoings of the past or my own inactions. But I firmly believe that the only way to irradiate racism is to do so with knowledge, so I pass this on to the world in hopes that it makes a small difference and one that can help make change long after my lungs can no longer hold breath.

Acknowledgments

First and foremost, I would like to thank my wife, Amber Barker, for her undying love, emotional support, and unwavering belief in me for helping to make this project possible.

Thank you to my institution, Texas Woman's University, for giving me this opportunity.

I thank J. Dustin Williams, Jason "Doc Holiday" Lulos, and Madison Brown for their hours dedicated to reading my manuscript to eliminate errors and suggestions on how to improve.

Finally, I want to thank my loving family, Larry, Faith, and Julie Barker for their unwavering support throughout this entire process.

"A fellow prisoner," "Like a dog," and "There is nothing" by Keiho Soga, translated by Jiro and Kay Nakano, used by permission Joyce Miyamoto.

"Alcatraz," "For Ace," and "Sweat Lodge—The Afterwards" by Peter Blue Cloud from *Clans of Many Nations*, used by permission of White Pine Press. Copyright © 1995.

"Blood of a Warrior" and "Voices in the Water" from *A Scar upon Our Voice* by Robin Coffee. Copyright © 2005. University of New Mexico Press, 2005.

"Cities behind Glass" and "The Truth Is" reprinted from *Seeing through the Sun*. Copyright © 1985 by Linda Hogan. Published by the University of Massachusetts Press.

Yamada, Mitsuye. "Cincinnati." In *Camp Notes and Other Writings*. New Brunswick: Rutgers University Press, 1998. Copyright © 1998 by Mitsuye Yamada. Reprinted by permission of Rutgers University Press.

Yamada, Mitsuye. "The Question of Loyalty." In *Camp Notes and Other Writings*. New Brunswick: Rutgers University Press, 1998. Copyright © 1998 by Mitsuye Yamada. Reprinted by permission of Rutgers University Press.

Chapter One

Traditionally, literary trauma theory, which originated from deconstruction, examines literature through a close reading and demonstrates ways in which the representation works against the theme of trauma within the literature. Other analyses of literature through the literary trauma lens examine the author in hopes of gaining a better understanding of the text and the author (chapter 1 of Cassie Premo Steele, *We Heal from Memory: Sexton, Lorde, Anzaldúa, and the Poetry of Witness*, immediately comes to mind). The present study looks to build off the reader response approach to demonstrate how poetry can work toward building community and encouraging empowerment by establishing collectives of people who may share similar stories and experiences connected to trauma. Rather than demonstrating how the poetry may fail or trying to establish what traumatic events the speaker (or poet, in some studies) may have encountered and the significance thereof, this study focuses on how the reader may find community with the ideas represented within the poem. Many times, individuals who have suffered from trauma isolate themselves from others, which is not always conducive to their overall well-being. By understanding that they are not alone in their experience, and by being able to read the ideas of a speaker who may be sharing their experience, a reader may find solace and comfort in the writings, even when they are not overtly comforting. Furthermore, with the violent events that seem to be more common in our society, like mass shootings, and permeation of readily available technology in which to record such traumatic events, it would seem only logical that not only are more people being exposed to traumatic events in varying degrees, but more people may be traumatized than ever before. It should be noted that this study is not abandoning the idea of close reading poems through the examination of literary trauma theory, but this type of analysis is not the focus. Furthermore, this study will examine the existence of ambivalence within poetry written about trauma.

The study of paradox in poetry is nothing new. Cleanth Brooks, in *The Well Wrought Urn*, takes great care to discuss the paradox that exists in the language of poetry. This paradox, comprised most commonly by contradictions, is a common aspect of poetry. Of the idea of paradox, within his chapter dedicated to paradox within language, he discussed the poetry of William Wordsworth (among others) and demonstrates paradox of the nun in "It is a Beauteous Evening, Calm and Free" and how the nun is said to be "breathless." Of this he says, "the evening is like a nun breathless with adoration. The adjective 'breathless' suggests tremendous excitement; and yet the evening is not only quiet but *calm*. There is no final contradiction, to be sure: it is *that* kind of calm and *that* kind of excitement, and the two states may well occur together. . . . He must work by contradiction and qualification."[1] Brooks states that the poet must use this type of paradox because there is no term that would suffice in replicating this type of description of the night.[2]

This is not the subject matter of this study.

Paradox deals with statements that although maybe self-contradictory are true. As above, the evening is both exciting and calm, which does not seem logical, but such an experience can and does exist. Ambivalence means something similar yet vastly different. Whereas paradox focuses mainly on statements and proposition, ambivalence resides in one's attitudes or emotions. To be sure, ambivalence revolves around contradiction, yet it is not always paradoxical. This should not be confused with ambiguity, which has more to do with uncertainty and multiple ways of interpreting. What is more, ambivalence is psychological.

José Bleger's *Symbiosis and Ambiguity: A Psychoanalytical Study*, published in 1967, has recently been translated into English for the first time, which allows its contributions to psychology to be understood by a much wider audience. In the final three chapters of his text, he reviews the history of ambivalence and discusses its use in the works of Freud. He beautifully and succinctly traces ambiguity from Eugen Bleuler to Freud through Melanie Klein and Ronald Fairbairn. Ambivalence is a psychological idea, whose long history stems back to Spinoza, was introduced to the symptoms of schizophrenia by Bleuler, and in the topic of Jose Bleger's text *Symbiosis and Ambiguity*, Bleger warns:

> The term ambivalence must be reserved for case in which two antinomic behaviours coincide in relation to the same object at the same time: there may be two opposite attitudes, affects, ideas or tendencies, as long as they have not arrived at a synthesis or working-through of the conflict. When, as in the case of schizophrenics, they do not necessarily bring together "the different aspects of

a problem," as Bleuler puts it, then we cannot use the concept of ambivalence but only that of *divalence* [author's emphasis]. This phenomenon may present not only in pathology for, as Bleuler notes, "even under normal conditions, synthesis may be omitted." (p. 375). This divalence is developmentally prior to ambivalence. The latter is, then, inevitably characterized by the simultaneous or joint presence (in relation to the same object at the same time) of two contradictory terms. If the presentation alternates (in time) it is divalence, the same occurs when they are directly at the same object, although for the subject they are different objects whose antinomic qualities have not yet been integrated. When this integration, synthesis or working-through has been reached, we still cannot designate it as ambivalent. In short, ambivalence always means conflict, whether it is conscious or unconscious ambivalence.[3]

The idea of ambivalence is brought up here not to suggest any type of schizophrenia, but to illuminate the ambivalence presented with trauma literature and how the use of ambivalence is not only a characteristic of poetry but one of survivors of trauma as discussed by Jerg-Bretzke et al. in such studies as "Emotional Ambivalence and Post-Traumatic Stress Disorder (PTSD) in Soldiers during Military Operations."

In the same year as this English translation (2013), Jerg-Bretzke et al. found that a correlation exists between emotional ambivalence and post-traumatic stress disorder. The study found that German soldiers who displayed emotional ambivalence before being deployed were more likely to experience more severe symptoms of PTSD. As such, the study suggests that emotional ambivalence may be a good predictor of psychological burden. Although this is a potentially valuable study for clinical psychology and may help predict who may be most impacted by psychological burdens, this may not be a great surprise to those who read and study literature written about or connected to trauma. In fact, a great deal of literature exists that presents ambivalence within the poem, especially in poetry that is alluding to trauma. Although poets and other writers have been doing this for years, it seems to have gone relatively unnoticed.

To be clear, the study mentioned above is not suggesting that emotional ambivalence is a result of a traumatic incident. It is suggesting that the correlation could be a good indicator for predicting. This finding has implications for our study of English. Just as writers have used various recognized techniques to represent the unrepresentable, like isolation and repetition, they have also been using ambivalence unbeknownst to many observers, and perhaps themselves. The use of these motifs aid in the presentation and discussion of trauma, some of which may be shown through the speaker, herself. Jerg-Bretzke et al. state that their study "is the first to examine how ambivalence among soldiers with regard to the expression of their emotions affects the occurrence of PTSD after deployment in a crisis region."[4] What they found was that "the correlations between emotional ambivalence on the one hand and the specific post-traumatic stress on the other are not only statistically significant but may be relevant as risk factors."[5] As a result, "Soldiers who are unable to express their feelings in a social context (competence ambivalence) or do not want to do so (effect ambivalence) thus have an increased risk of experiencing the deployment as stressful and burdensome and to experience symptoms of post-traumatic stress disorder."[6] We must be cautious in that this study was the first of its kind and also contained a small sample size; however, what it suggests is that those who present ambivalence before a traumatic event are more likely to be traumatized. Therefore, it is not surprising to find elements of ambivalence in traumatic poetry.

Ambivalence, which may be at times paralytic, can be a product of abjection, which Kristeva identifies as "what disturbs identity, system, order."[7] Various aspects of trauma, such as repetition, abjection, and ambivalence are found within literature about trauma as it is presented in a way that is performative in order to inform the reader in an extralinguistic way. Much like Kristeva's *Powers of Horror*, as well as Lacan and Derrida, writers of literary trauma texts often utilize the text in a performative manner to relay extralinguistic elements that perhaps cannot be aptly conveyed in language itself. Although it could be argued that poetry has, perhaps, always worked in this manner, poetry dealing with trauma does more so.

Literary trauma theory has the ability to examine the history of different groups and the traumatic events that have taken place in the past that still impact the people of that particular group. The traumatic events endured fundamentally defy a satisfactory definition or representation—otherwise, they would not be traumatic—forcing writers to utilize other means of signification within their writing. Literary trauma theory recognizes the attempt by writers to voice the stories, not only of those traumas but of those who have been oppressed, marginalized, and silenced throughout history and may continue to be today. This book works to expand upon previous studies of literature that have used literary trauma theory as a guide to better understand the literature and how it may impact the reader. This book echoes the arguments of theorists like Ron Eyerman, Neil Smelser, Susan Brison, and Luminita M. Dragulescu who argue that focus needs to be placed on different historical, cultural, and racial traumas. In fact, this study is responding to the call for more examination of minority literature by theorists like Stef Craps who stated "the founding texts of the field (including Caruth's own work) largely fail to live up to this promise of cross-cultural ethical engagement."[8] Furthermore, one of the ways it fails is that "they marginalize or ignore traumatic experiences of non-Western or minority cultures."[9] In response, his study focuses on the trauma within minority literatures and examines how these types of literature can be used to empower people over oppression, as well as focuses on poetry, which is a genre that has been neglected to be amply explored.

This study engages the poetry of three distinct American minority cultures who have endured traumatic pasts and whose poetry, although to different extents, encouraged empowerment through the engagement of this trauma. From the very outset, I believe it beneficial to acknowledge that although this study does engage three very different cultures, it does not by any means fully represent the poetry of those cultures, of their particular period, or even of the poet him- or herself. This study does examine selected poets because of their ability to draw on a tradition of lyric expressivism and expressive emotionalism. I admit that the sample of poets and the sample of poems are relatively small, but the goal of this study is not to examine the evolution of literary trauma theory or engagement with massive stressors for an entire culture. Instead, this study has sought out to expand upon literary trauma theory and reorient trauma theory to examine poetry, but more specifically, poetry of American minority writers. Most significantly, I would argue, this study finds the importance that engaging massive stressors and historic traumas has with encouraging empowerment among those who have been oppressed and denigrated, as well as discussing abjection, ambivalence, and the performative role of literary devices. Additionally, as stated early on, the analysis of the poetry will deviate from a more traditional examination and utilize a reader response lens in conjunction with literary trauma theory.

In order to understand and discuss the effects of trauma on many American minorities, the focus moves away from the direct impact of trauma on individuals to the effect of historical trauma on subsequent generations. This study will examine three groups who have legacies of trauma that transcend the generation directly affected by trauma and who contend with the aftereffects of the traumas. The poets of this study are working toward empowerment as they articulate the traumas that resonate within their poetry. Although the speakers in some of the Japanese American poetry move toward empowerment in a more subdued manner, the speakers within the poetry of the Black Arts Movement and the American Indian Movement call for radical change, not only against the white oppressor but also for the formation of new groups and new ways of presenting this empowerment in the artwork. A study of this type of poetry is much in line with the manner that literary trauma studies have been gravitating. In her article "Trauma and Power in Postcolonial Literary Studies," Irene Visser discusses the limits and trajectories of literary trauma theory in the field of postcolonial studies. One trajectory she discusses is how "social activism and political protest may be integral to the aftermath of the trauma of colonization and decolonization. In this respect, resistance and resilience are to be seen not merely as responses of individuals but more importantly, as part of a communal process of living and working through trauma."[10] The poetry of these political movements does just that. As a response to both historical and sometimes direct trauma, the speakers of the poems work toward resistance to the oppressive white superstructure while also working on a community and culture that was uniquely their own.

In her reading of Stef Craps, Visser notes very astutely that a change is necessary in postcolonial study. She states, "There is, then, in postcolonial studies currently a clear call for a new model for reading, understanding, and interpreting trauma that would enable more differentiated, and more culturally and historically specific notions, and would also provide ways of reading collective trauma."[11] Visser correctly notes the need to utilize knowledge from the disciplines of sociology and anthropology, discussing the contributions of Jeffery Alexander and Kai Erikson. Although I am in agreement with these ideas, more focus needs to be placed on historical trauma, and the disciplines of sociology and anthropology are perfectly in line for such an exploration. In order to have stronger understanding of trauma in postcolonial writings, it is imperative that scholars understand the significance of the historical trauma. Fortunately, this is an area that has been explored by scholars like Kaplan, Brave Heart, and others.

Since E. Ann Kaplan's book in 2005, theorists have been exploring the effects of trauma on people who were not directly involved in the traumatic event. Such indirect effects are known as "vicarious trauma" and are outlined by Kaplan as:

> 2) direct observation of another's trauma (bystander, one step removed); 3) visually mediated trauma (i.e. moviegoer, viewing trauma on film or other media, two steps removed); 4) reading a trauma narrative and constructing visual image of semantic data (news reader, three steps removed); 5) hearing a patient's trauma narrative.[12]

Understanding the variations of proximity to the experiences as related to trauma can benefit our overall comprehension of trauma and how it can be identified and can be useful when discussing trauma as it relates to the literature of different poets. By doing so, we can also observe how trauma has affected the people of a certain ethnic group (as vicarious trauma) or the individual speaker, both understood in a larger historical framework.

It is clear that Kaplan has gone to great lengths outlining various proximities of trauma. From this one can understand how trauma may affect a particular group both presently and as a result of trauma that has occurred in the past.

Such a comprehension of the various proximities inherent with the effects of trauma allows for a greater insight into how trauma may be entwined within the culture of a particular ethnicity. Antonius C. G. M. Robben Marcelo and M. Suarez-Orozco state in their essay "Management of Collective Trauma":

> Massive traumas do not just nestle themselves in the victim's inner world: they are transmitted within the family and across generations. Gample introduces the concept of "radioactivity" in her reflection on social violence to describe how traumatic experiences can continue to do emotional damage to future generations. A "radioactive" leakage occurs when parents' debilitating traumatic memories affect their children. The children of survivors often internalize incomprehensible fears and anxieties which undermine a healthy separation from inner and outer reality.[13]

Vicarious, or historical, trauma such as this often extends beyond the familial setting and is found in the shared experiences created by a particular group—for example, through stories. Examples of collective or historical trauma are found in the recounting of familial histories by African Americans of the traumatic experiences of ancestors at the hands of slaveholders, through stories of traumas inflicted through the Civil Rights Movement, as well as traumatic encounters felt presently. These types of historical traumas, as well as examples of individual traumatic experiences, are manifested within the poetry of not only some African American poets, but many, if not all, oppressed cultures. The poetry written by these poets allow for anyone, regardless of culture, to gain an understanding of these experiences and demonstrates literature's universality, which is not a new idea, but one especially important to the literature studied here. The fact that trauma many times isolates an individual or a group is combated by the universality of literature, thereby allowing the poet and other members of a cultural group that suffer through trauma, both direct and vicarious, a means to form a community, not only with one another, but with people outside of their culture who may not understand their struggle.

Scholars like Maria Yellow Horse Brave Heart pay particular attention to the legacies of traumatic stressors and the impact that these have across generations. Historic trauma is defined by Brave Heart in her article "The Historical Trauma Response among Natives and Its Relationship to Substance Abuse: A Lakota Illustration." Brave Heart defines historic trauma as the "cumulative emotional and psychological wounding, over the lifespan and across generations, emanating from massive group trauma experiences."[14] In addition to historical trauma, Brave Heart also discusses the idea of historic trauma response, which she defines as "the constellation of features in reaction to this [historic] trauma. The HTR [historic trauma response] may include substance abuse as a vehicle for attempting to numb the pain associated with trauma."[15] This type of substance abuse, used in order to numb the pain from trauma, is not a phenomenon unique to Native Americans, but it is quite significant when one considers the difficulties with substance abuse that plague the Native American population.[16] The mention and discussion of drinking is apparent within the poetry of many Native American poets. For example, Coffee's small collection of poetry *A Scar upon Our Voice* contains no less than eleven poems that refer to alcohol or alcoholism. Drug and alcohol references appear in the work of many African American and Asian American poets as well.

Brave Heart continues with her discussion of historical trauma response by discussing how it also includes other destructive behavior beyond substance abuse. Brave Heart states that historical trauma response "often includes other types of self-destructive behavior, suicidal thoughts and gestures, depression, anxiety, low self-esteem, anger, and difficulty recognizing and expressing emotions."[17] These types of behaviors and feelings are found readily in the poetry of all three cultures to be discussed in this study but are readily found in the poetry of all cultures. In addition, Brave Heart stipulates and refers to previous articles published by her that argue that "associated with HTR [historical trauma response] is historical unresolved grief that accompanies the trauma; this grief may be considered impaired, delayed, fixated, and/or disenfranchised."[18] The idea of unresolved grief is of great importance because it articulates, perhaps more directly, the sentiments and emotions found within a great deal of poetry with elements of trauma. To state that the poetry of a historically traumatized culture exemplifies the characteristics of historically unresolved grief is more psychologically viable because the characteristics associated with unresolved grief are more readily apparent than the characteristics of trauma, especially those of post-traumatic stress disorder (PTSD). Ideas such as these presented by Brave Heart are necessary to gain a greater understanding of how historical trauma continues to affect different individuals and the emergence of these struggles as they are found in poetry.

Although trauma is apparent in other genres, such as prose and film, poetry differs in various characteristics from other genres, especially in its healing ability due to its close connection with emotion. Trauma theorists such as Cathy Caruth and Dominique LaCapra have pointed toward the benefit for the writer of literature dealing with trauma as a means of coping with the trauma. Trauma tends to be relived by victims rather than remembered, and the full effect of the trauma, whether historical or direct, individual or group, is never fully comprehended at the time of the trauma. Thus, by reliving the trauma, the person is attempting to gain an understanding of the events. With this in mind, it is very easy to see why people who place great emotional emphasis in their writing, such as poets often do, would be inclined to discuss stressors and traumas occurring in their life or in their community.

With traumas of larger scale, such as the Holocaust and slavery, the impact of the trauma is passed on for many generations and felt by a large group of people. Just as telling one's trauma is a means of coping for an individual, a similar beneficial coping response can be found in the reading of trauma by other survivors whereby it allows survivors to have a sense of community and an ability, much like in writing, to examine trauma from a different perspective. By realizing that the traumatic event occurred in the past (regardless if the trauma is direct or vicarious), the writer and reader are able to conceptualize the fact that the trauma is in the past and the future is available to them. In addition, poetry, unlike other forms of writing, allows for a unique connection to trauma due to the emphasis on poetic devices that are similar to forms of traumatic memory. Because traumatic memory and poetry share many of the same characteristics, and because of the survivor's need to tell, it is logical to find poetry as one of the most appropriate methods to tell about trauma.

The focus on trauma in poetry by Cassie Premo Steele and Walter Kalaidjian has greatly benefited the field by identifying how trauma can be represented in poetry and various techniques a poet may employ in order to represent trauma within their poetry. Kalaidjian, in his book *The Edge of Modernism*, makes great progress in finding the benefit of analyzing poetry through a traumatic lens, and in my study I wish to expand on his vein of thinking. Kalaidjian states in his book:

> I wish to propose a new consideration of how the agency of the letter in poetic discourse testifies to the truth of traumatic reference in ways that make special claims on us in excess of our normal roles as authors and readers. Although literature's fictive grounding in the figurative use of language would hardly seem fitted to disclosures of referential truth, I would argue that the poetry of generations witness—precisely as a linguistic event—manifest its forces in revolutionary ways. What is properly an unspeakable or "buried" trauma in the ancestor, no matter how distant, appears like a ghost haunting the symptomatic actions, phobias, "puppet emotions," hallucinations, and—most telling—the "staged words" or *cryptonyms* of the decedents.[19]

I agree with Kalaidjian that historical trauma can be manifested in the poetry of subsequent generations. The focus of this study is to apply this concept to poetry produced by three distinct American cultures and examine the way poetry has aided in empowering the writers and cultures. An overlying theme present within the poetry of these cultures is the feeling of displacement, ambivalence, and abjection. This feeling, as this study shall show, is common within the poetry dealing with trauma and is a common feeling of many who face traumatic stressors, either within their own life, or as they work through historical trauma as members of a minoritized culture.

Furthering these ideas, Steele states that the value of applying a literary trauma theory lens to poetry resides in how poetry allows for a unique insight that is dissimilar than what can be gained by any other genre or art form. According to Steele, "Poetry allows us to witness as survivors to having survived and to witness to others' survival: poetry, like trauma, takes images, feelings, rhythms, sounds, and the physical sensations of the body as evidence."[20] Steele also reminds us that "trauma is not recorded narratively, but, as many researchers have found, is recorded as images and feelings. It is poetry—with its visual images, metaphors, sounds, rhythms, and emotional impact—that can give voice to having survived."[21] Unlike typical prose, which usually attempts a type of completion, poetry allows an individual to express a portion of a narrative or a fragment in time and does so unapologetically. Postmodern literature and art are filled with fragmentation, in much the same way trauma is often recorded; however, it is within modern poetry that we find this type of fragmentation most predominantly. In addition, as Steele has discussed, it is precisely in the poetic devices ("visual images, metaphors, sounds, [and] rhythms"[22]) that trauma is most truly represented because it is very similar to the way it is recorded within the mind of the survivor. Steele's focus within her text is upon the poet rather than the speaker of the poem, which can, at times, be the same, yet I have reservations about trusting the poet as speaker.

I would stipulate that when one examines a poem, the person being examined in reference to trauma is the speaker and not the poet him- or herself. It would be easy to examine an Amiri Baraka poem and desire to examine trauma as it may have affected Baraka, but we must be clear that it is the speaker being examined, not the poet. When we take vicarious trauma into consideration, however, the difference between the poet and the speaker may be minimal, as long as it can be deduced that the speaker is of the same ethnicity and, thus, may have shared similar experiences in regard to vicarious trauma. As long as it can be deduced that the speaker and the poet are of the same ethnicity, we can then understand that the voice is *a* representative (and definitely not *the* representative) of the specific group. The speaker may present feelings shared by some members of the group, but not the group's as a whole, and may allow an insight into the massive stressors, traumas, and feelings that may be shared by a large number of people. We must also be mindful that vicarious trauma affects different cultures because of the experiences the people of that culture's ancestors encountered and the way the community coped with the trauma. This type of vicarious trauma is also known as historic trauma. Although coping with trauma is often an individual practice, it is also a response that occurs in familial or larger group settings; thus, in some situations the differences between the poet and the speaker of the poem may be minimal because they are both hypothetically speaking from the same community, and may, therefore, be encountering similar experiences in regard to historical trauma.

More studies need to focus on literary trauma theory being applied to multiethnic poetry, especially given the incredibly violent, hate-filled, and divisive climate of the United States throughout our history (and presently). Many theorists have discussed the importance of understanding cultural and historical memory and the impact that these traumas may have on individuals within those cultures. In Luminita M. Dragulescu's article "The Middle Passage and Race-Based Trauma" she beautifully and succinctly traces the history of cultural trauma, beginning with Maurice Halbwachs's *On Collective Memory* (1925) and ending with Stef Craps's contemporary ideas. She concludes:

> Historical race trauma is sustained by the delayed recognition of black history and the systemic indifference to the consequences of a history of racial violence. In acknowledging race trauma, it is imperative to establish the causal links among racist discourses, cultural contexts, and the socio-political framework that generate and propagate trauma. Narratives of trauma are located somewhere between the compulsion to tell and the suppression of what must be told.[23]

Her idea applies not only to African Americans and African American literature, but to many different cultures of the United States and beyond. The lack of education and propagation of racism, hate, and bigotry have resulted in the continuation of trauma within many different races and cultures. Unfortunately, people are continually inundated with such propaganda through such mediums as social media and cable news as well as the hate rhetoric that now permeates politics, again. As Dragulescu states later in the same article, "As long as racist discourses still define a society, they act as a catalyst of trauma both through the reenactment of the traumatic past and through the present experience of failed inter-racial rapports."[24]

A method to combat such ignorance is through education, which can ultimately lead to empowerment. Furthermore, as Bilyana Vanyova Kostova articulates in her astutely written article "'Time to Write Them Off'? Impossible Voices and the Problem of Representing Trauma in *The Virgin Suicides*," "Not only is narrative meant to arouse empathy in the readers but it also serves as a means to work through traumatic experiences and their memories, wrapping them in meaning, and helping victims of trauma to cope with the overwhelming events from their past and their haunting consequences."[25] As an educator who has spent his career teaching at predominately African American and Hispanic universities, it is evident that teaching students literature from their own culture has a dramatic effect. Not only do these students thirst for knowledge about their own culture (because we have systematically removed it from curricula in the public education system), but many of these students have faced trauma directly or from cultural/historic trauma. In 2017, two of my own students were shot and murdered in separate incidents. They can obviously not speak of their trauma, but countless others are impacted by situations like this. By allowing students to read literature that engages trauma, like that of the Black Arts Movement, people are able to learn about a history that is often rarely spoken of, but they are also exposed to it in a personal and emotional manner. This is part of the power of literature and something that should never be forgotten.

As Kalaidjian and Steele have demonstrated in their texts, the application of literary trauma theory to poetry can be quite fruitful. Although various art forms lend themselves readily to expression, poetry typically lends itself more readily to expressing emotions and confessions. Unlike other forms of writing, poetry typically places great emphasis on imagery. By using imagery, the poet can elicit an emotional response from her audience that may evoke feelings of fear, helplessness, sadness, anger, or other feelings associated with trauma. In addition, poetry also utilizes the idea of fragmentation more than other types of writings. Many times, a poem will present an incident within a person's life or an emotional experience of a person rather than the much more in-depth narratives presented in most other forms of creative writing. Finally, poems often present their ideas more indirectly than other forms of writing by using literary devices like metaphors and similes. Furthermore, the general population often views poems as being difficult to understand and as having stratified meanings; thus, the indirectness of poetry is well recognized, not only by those who study poetry, but also by society. As a result, it is not difficult for many poets to translate traumatic memory into poems because of characteristics they both share.

The use of imagery, metaphor, and the expression of emotion in poetry are important when we consider Nanette Auerhahn and Dori Laub's discussion of the various forms of traumatic memory in "Intergenerational Memory of the Holocaust." Several of the ten forms of traumatic memory they discuss are akin to poetry as a genre as well as many poetic devices, which makes the telling of the trauma easily translated into poems. Auerhahn and Laub's discussion of traumatic memory is, I believe, intrinsic to the idea of historic trauma and the manner in which it manifests through many generations. In order to gain a greater understanding of the different forms of traumatic knowledge, it is worth discussing not only the forms of traumatic knowledge that are pertinent to this study, but Auerhahn and Laub's discussion of traumatic memory itself:

Traumatic memory thus entails a process of evolution that requires several generations in which to play itself out. We initially understood this to be the result of conflicts arising from the paradoxical yoking of the compulsions to remember and to know trauma with the equally urgent needs to forget and not to know it (Auerhahn and Laub, 1990), but now to see the situation as infinitely more complex. For along with any conscious or unconscious needs to know or not to know exists deficits in our abilities to grasp trauma, name it, recall it, and paradoxically, forget it.[26]

Auerhahn and Laub outline several forms of traumatic memory, many of which are pertinent to this study as they are so akin to poetry.

The first type of memories that lend themselves to poetry are screen memories. Auerhahn and Laub build off of Freud's idea of screen memories, from 1899, and, like Freud, are a type of alternative or false memory. Screen memories (the second type of memory discussed by Auerhahn and Laub) are generated because of not knowing, which is the first type of memory they discuss. Not knowing is, just as the name implies, the blocking of memories due to their traumatic nature. Screen memories fill this gap by "the creation of an alternative, possibly false, self that screens over the absence of memory. Such a path can readily lead to mythmaking or the creation of false memories that constitute another form of knowing that goes beyond the first level's awareness of an absence of the creation of a fiction that covers over that absence."[27] Obviously, the creation of fictional memories can easily lend itself to a variety of art forms, with poetry being just one outlet. The significance of this form of memory is not that it is unique to poetry, but this fictional telling is a means of coping for many survivors. Auerhahn and Laub address this, stating, "Fictionalization is an inherent part of any attempt to recall trauma, for the truth of trauma can never be fully recaptured. Instead, we have found most true trauma stories to be factually accurate in many ways and factually inaccurate in many ways, containing the facts as perceived (an arduous, incomplete, and interpretive process) and as defended against."[28] This is incredibly important to note because poetry, like many arts, allows the survivor to tell their trauma without actually telling the exact trauma. In other words, the survivor tells of *a* trauma, which does not necessarily have to be *their* trauma, and allows for a release, if we recall the survivor's intrinsic need to tell. Auerhahn and Laub continue by stating, "In many works of art that attempt to give voice to, or master, trauma, there often is a 'lie,' a distortion, covering over the as yet unworked through and unknown aspect of trauma."[29] This allows the poet to examine this trauma while it is still being worked through and provides an outlet through a mask of fiction. Screen memories, as has been stated, are easily adapted into a variety of art forms; thus, it is not surprising to find them appearing in poetry. However, other types of memories discussed by Auerhahn and Laub that are more easily represented by poetry than other forms of writing are "fragments," and "trauma as metaphor."

Fragments or fragmented memories are important for discussions of poetry related to its form. Although a great deal of postmodern art and writing is fragmented in nature, the very art form of poetry is oftentimes a fragment. Auerhahn and Laub state, "Remembering involves the retention of parts of a lived experience in such a way that they are decontextualized and no longer meaningful. The individual has an image, sensation, or isolated thought, but does not know with what it is connected, what it means, or what to do with it."[30] Unlike most novels, short stories, or dramas, which usually contain an element of character development and a narrative structure, poems often provide only a glimpse into a person's life or a scene, which is presented because it is important or significant to the speaker. In order to present such a fragment, poetry is the perfect genre to portray a fragmented memory because the art form allows for such disconnectedness. More so than other forms of writing, poems are given a great deal of leeway in regard to their format, their disconnectedness from reality, and ambiguity, each of which are not only acceptable, but are many times expected.

Fragmentation and disconnectedness may also take the form of images or a series of images. Because memory is often recorded as images, it is of little surprise that poets who desire to convey trauma in their poems may utilize images within their poem that evoke response from the reader. Poetry by African Americans may use the imagery of slavery, plantations, whips, nooses, the railroad, or rivers, all of which have had great significance within African American culture. These images are loaded; thus, their use is not simply to recall African American heritage, but African American trauma heritage. Additionally, Japanese American poets may use the images of internment camps recalling the Japanese internment camps of World War II. Native American poets may use imagery of atrocities of the past, displacement from the land, and even present themselves as warriors to fight against the oppressor, recalling the past in their metaphor or metonym. These images are not only used to evoke past traumas but become symbols of the past traumas. As the following examination of Komunyakaa's poem illustrates, these symbols become intrinsic to the semantic quality of the poem as a vehicle of meaning.

In his poem "Reflections,"[31] Komunyakaa presents the very loaded image of a noose that is used for suicide in the poem, but more importantly, the *symbol* of the noose brings forth thoughts of lynching and the trauma associated with the horrific acts perpetrated against African Americans in the not-so-distant past. The poem discusses an African American man (line 2) standing beneath a noose. Although it is not apparent whether he is committing suicide or being lynched, the speaker is obviously distressed. The poem

"Reflections" begins with the line "In the day's mirror" (line 1), which is significant in several ways. First, it is evident that there is a connection between the speaker and the man who is dying, as, at the end of the poem, the speaker discusses the reader's feet in his shoes. The fact that the speaker places the reader in the man's position is indicative that the situation could just as easily have happened to the reader, thereby eliciting empathy and the idea that this is not an uncommon occurrence. Secondly, the fact that we are given the image of the day in a mirror presents the event as if it were a reflection, thereby placing the idea that this event, although happening in the present for the speaker, could also be a flashback being lived and/or a reoccurring incident that has taken place in the past as well.

These symbols are reflective techniques used by the poet to show how the traumatic history can affect others as they look back upon their culture's history. The noose is an image and symbol that has a strong traumatic connection for African Americans because of lynching in the past. The use of this symbol calls upon that past within the poem and allows the reader to experience the feelings of the past without the speaker mentioning these feelings explicitly. The poem demonstrates that the death of the person in the poem affects the speaker to the point that he or she is connected with the man who is dying, thus demonstrating the impact of historic trauma in this metaphor where the dying of one man, especially through the powerfully symbolic method (noose), directly affects others. By speaking in second person, the poem creates an intimacy with the man in the poem and the reader. Although there is a strong emotional connection with the man in the poem and the speaker, the speaker is also attempting to draw a connection with the reader so that the reader understands that this traumatic historic affects her as well.

The images of lynching used in "Reflections" are a good example; however, Komunyakaa uses this technique in many other poems. In his poem "Annabelle,"[32] the opening lines contain the word "hangs" and the second stanza ends with the line "All to do with rope & blood" (line 7). Similar Komunyakaa poems like "Family Tree"[33] call upon images of slavery such as "a whip \ across my back," (lines 2–3) at the start of the poem, thus setting the tone for a poem where the speaker describes some of the hardships the family members had to endure during slavery in America. Komunyakaa evokes images of oppression, lynching, and slavery with images such as a chain (line 12), cotton field (line 24), slave (line 33), hanging trees (line 36), chopping cotton (line 49), and mule plowing (line 51) to mention just a few. These images within the poems force the reader to realize the traumatic history that the speaker is presenting and that remains in his or her mind.

The poem "Reflections" also utilizes poetic techniques such as very short lines in order to propel the reader along, creating an anxiety within the poem by making the reader's eyes move quickly down the page. This anxiety is reinforced by Komunyakaa's use of line breaks, which force the reader to speculate at the end of the line. An example of anxiety produced by a line break occurs in line four of the poem, which discusses the fear generated as the reader has witnessed the event to the point that the reader is said to tremble. This is then able to generate a feeling of uneasiness in multiple ways. First, the poem is placed in the second person, making it very intimate, but in this line, this placement into the second person is especially troubling because the line tells us that we are a "witness" (line 4) then stops. We are unsure of what we are witnessing and are forced to pause while our eyes move to the next line. The fact that the line begins with the word trembling reinforces the feeling of uneasiness because the word could represent a number of negative emotional manifestations. The trembling is tied to the personification of the lines that were discussing the reader seeing a black man beneath a noose (line 3). At this point in the poem, we are still not completely sure what is occurring and have been given mainly images with which to work. Because of the confusion, the anxiety is magnified and Komunyakaa is able to transfer a feeling of uneasiness to the reader through a combination of narrative and poetic devices rather than telling the reader that they need to feel uneasy.

Komunyakaa's use of traumatic figurative language, the symbolism used in this poem, and the anxiety created through short lines are typical for poets exploring trauma in their poems. Furthermore, Komunyakaa is able to represent trauma within the first six lines by providing mostly images and very little narrative. Traumatic memory, as has been outlined by Steele, as well as several trauma theorists, is recorded as a collection of images rather than a story; therefore, this first portion of the poem with the collection of images, especially the noose, is very representational of trauma. A feeling of helplessness follows as the "you" within the poem attempts to stop what is occurring but is unable to because your voice will not reach him. While Komunyakaa's poem presented here is an exemplar of common tropes used to present trauma to the reader, he is only one example of many. Numerous poets utilize the placement of words on the page in order to maximize the feelings of uneasiness that can be evoked, as well as the placement of line breaks and stanza breaks in order to create anxiety. When used alongside images that are particularly traumatic for a certain group, like a noose for African Americans, these poetic techniques become very effective.

As has been examined, the use of screen memories as described by Auerhahn and Laub, although perhaps unbeknownst to the poets, are easily identifiable in poetry discussing trauma. Many of the poetic devices used within the poems are extenuations of the traumatic memories outlined. Traumatic memories, such as screen memories, fragmentation, and disconnectedness, often manifest into images and symbols within the poems. As has been stated, understanding traumatic memory is intrinsic to the study of traumatic history and how such trauma is communicated within poetry. Screen memories allow survivors, and for our discussion, poets, to fictionalize the traumas that they explore in order to discuss that which is unrepresentable. Komunyakaa is not the first, nor is he alone, in presenting elements of trauma, not only in images but also in themes, within his poetry. The images of traumatic events are often used when poets use traumatic figurative language within their poem in order to discuss trauma in their past or trauma and stressors that they are currently encountering.

Screen memories are generated because of not knowing, which is the first type of memory discussed. The second type of memory that is pertinent to this study is trauma as metaphor. Trauma as metaphor "is the use of the imagery and language of massive psychological trauma as metaphor and vehicle for developmental conflict."[34] Trauma as metaphor is similar to types of memory known as witnessed narrative in that "the distance between event and witness is preserved, yet goes beyond (but paradoxically never reaches) the previous level of knowing in that an element of play vis-à-vis the event enters, enabling the event's use as a metaphor that has some latitude."[35] The survivor or, for our purpose, the speaker of the poem, utilizes metaphor, or other types of figurative language, in order to discuss an event that has happened to him or her, and uses the descriptions or specific words that are associated with a more traumatic event. Because the event is too painful or frightening to directly examine, traumatic metaphors are a type of displacement that the survivor uses in order to cope and discuss the trauma. Poets use traumatic figurative language when discussing or showing the trauma within their poems because, just as the event is too traumatic to discuss directly, poets may use traumatic figurative language as a means of both displacing the trauma and discussing it. Although a survivor may use a traumatic metaphor to displace the event in order to discuss it, poets utilize traumatic figurative language to grapple with representing what may be unrepresentable.

Auerhahn and Laub continue by stating:

> The imagery of trauma becomes more conscious, colorful, plastic, and variable than that found in other levels of knowing. It readily appears in free associations and in dream associations, and does not have to be inferred or drawn out from ingrained silent modes of action. There is a disengagement from the event and its legacy as the individual chooses only those aspects of the event that reverberate with his or her internal conflict. The developmental conflict, rather than the event, is paramount and is the moving force behind the search for an appropriate vehicle of expression; that is, the motive for this form of traumatic memory comes from the need to organize internal experience than, as with the previous forms, from a need to organize the external historical reality.[36]

Trauma as metaphor, or traumatic metaphor, is used primarily by individuals coping with historical stress. The developmental conflict being discussed by Auerhahn and Laub refers to the individuals coping with historical trauma that has fallen onto them from their parents, grandparents, or from their cultural heritage. Trauma is not something that can be worked through in one generation; thus, subsequent generations of people may be affected and utilize traumatic metaphors in order to comprehend, cope, and overcome the historic trauma, though implicitly this means that direct access to the trauma is impossible or undesired. Auerhahn and Laub give an example of a woman whose paternal grandparents were directly affected by the Holocaust. She describes events in her life by using imagery of the Holocaust. For example, during her tonsillectomy, she refers to her doctor as a Nazi surgeon.[37] Similar use of trauma as metaphor can be found in a poetic sense in Silvia Plath's poem "Daddy."[38] The speaker of Plath's poem describes her father as a Nazi and presents a great deal of Nazi imagery surrounding the speaker's father. Given that Plath's own father, Otto, was a first-generation German immigrant who died when Plath was only eight, mixing Holocaust metaphors with the trauma of losing her father is an excellent example of using trauma as metaphor in the form of traumatic figurative language. As may be apparent in the above example, the poet may utilize traumatic figurative language in order to discuss very stressful (although perhaps not traumatic) incidents within their life and intentionally recalling well-known traumatic events in order to inform the reader of their pain. Poets may also utilize traumatic figurative language to compare historic traumas to contemporary stresses, some of which may be traumatic, that still occur presently, as articulated by poets such as Robin Coffee who compares his speaker within some of his poems to Native American warriors, each of which fight oppression.

The use of traumatic figurative language can be subtle, with the speaker referencing images that may conjure images of an historic trauma, such as the noose used in Komunyakaa's poem, or they may appear more overt, as in Etheridge Knight's poem "Once on a Night in the Delta: A Report from Hell."[39] Knight's poem directly evokes the idea of slavery and compares it to current conditions (in 1981) that African Americans are facing. The poem is addressed and dedicated to Sterling Brown and gives an image of a Southern town that still suffers from the aftereffects of slavery. The poem begins by presenting images and names to inform the reader that the setting of the poem is in the South. The second stanza of the poem begins describing the difficult and stressful conditions that many face within the town where they live. In line seven the speaker indicates that people on both sides of the town are poor and tells that the town is "peopled by Blacks" (line 8). It is apparent that the people being spoken of in this poem are African American and poor. In line nine, the speaker states how the people in the town "now / pack pistols," (note the forward slashes here are included by the author and do not indicate line breaks) indicating that violence is a part of the lifestyle in this town. These images are important because they give an insight into the difficulty that the people of the town are facing and lead to the traumatic figurative language within the next stanza.

The third stanza of Knight's poem contains the traumatic figurative language. This traumatic figurative language overtly compares the conditions that African Americans are living in to that of their slave ancestors. Although the people who stand in lines for welfare, food stamps, and to vote are not chained physically as coffles of slaves once were, they are chained together in poverty and oppression. The speaker not only sees similarities with his present circumstances, but also utilizes the idea of slavery in order to present the stressors that he and his fellow townspeople are left to contend with on a daily basis. The impact of the stressors caused by poverty and violence, and the historical trauma that is still present within the lives of the townspeople, are physically manifested within the eyes of the people (lines 17–18). The townspeople are visibly suffering from emotional scars caused by stressors related to their poor economic situations. The line break between lines seventeen and eighteen is significant because the fourth stanza tells of how the suffering continues from Brown's day until the present. This is reinforced by the speaker as he directly addresses Brown and mentions Slim Greer (lines 20–21). Slim Greer is a reference to a character in Brown's poem "Slim Greer in Hell" written in the early 1930s. Given that Knight wrote his poem in 1981, it is evident that he believes the suffering that African Americans faced in the early 1930s is still present fifty years later. The idea of engaging with massive stressors as a result of traumatic events continuing for generations is underscored by the poet as he breaks the description of physical manifestations of distress into the third and fourth stanza. This idea that Mississippi is hell is a second use of traumatic figurative language in the poem and exists as an actual metaphor rather than a simile as the previous one. Both instances of traumatic figurative language utilize realistic trauma (slavery) and mythical trauma (hell) in order to describe the difficulties that the people of the speaker's town face.

By utilizing traumatic figurative language in the poem, the poet is able to tell of his or her trauma in order to cope with it, or to aid in building a community so that other members of his or her culture that are coping with these traumas may feel part of a community or at least less isolated. By doing so, the community can work toward empowerment of the group and work against the oppressor. As such, different cultures may present images or motifs that are unique to their culture within the traumatic figurative language or may draw upon images and motifs shared by many, such as ethnic slurs, to present or discuss their traumas. We also find images that the poets use in order to empower the reader and trauma. Robin Coffee uses the image of the warrior to inspire empowerment, Peter Blue Cloud calls upon traditions of the past for empowerment within the community by using images of traditional Native American dance, and Lucille Clifton and Robert Hayden use the image of runaway slaves. Additionally, there is the use of stanza breaks and line length in order to promote a feeling of anxiety by attempting to control the speed of how the poem is read or focusing the reader's attention to certain words.

Poetic articulations of trauma allow the poet to engage and articulate various stressors that they wish to articulate within their poem. For many poets, this engagement is a means to empower people within their culture and the need to mobilize for political gain within society. Discussion and recognition of current massive stressors and historic traumas have the ability to move people to action. These devices are important because of their use in poetry, and for this study, I find them to be most valuable because of their ability to engage with the trauma, the manner in which they mimic historic trauma response, and the manner in which we may gain a greater understanding into the speakers' distress. This is not an uncommon practice when using literary trauma theory to engage a text. Many studies that focus on trauma in literature focus a great deal on repetitions that exist within the literary work because repetition is a common response to trauma and easily identifiable in text. Many survivors of trauma repeat aspects or the entirety of the event that was traumatic in their life, in their mind, and, sometimes, in their literature. Literary trauma theorists make note of these elements of repetition in a literary work and discuss the correlation therein. As Dorothy Stringer says in the introduction to her book, *Not Even Past: Race, Historical Trauma, and Subjectivity in Faulkner, Larsen, and Van Vechten*, "Like the present work [her own], many other contributors in literary and cultural trauma studies begin analysis with the acknowledgement of repetition."[40] Stringer also makes note how literary trauma theory takes into account "what cannot be fully remembered, the illegible, the unspeakable, with a something-repeated, be it an image, a phrase, a metaphor, even a syllable or sound."[41] The present study does not wish to discount repetition or any of the other aspects that literary trauma theory examines in literature. Instead, my study looks to expand beyond these facets and examine traumatic memory and the role of emotion, most specifically in poetry, as well as ambivalence.

It would be foolish for us to assume the emotion expressed within all poems to be authentic; however, given the political and social climate surrounding some writers, as well as the historical trauma prevalent within our society, I believe it would be equally foolish to discount the emotions, anxieties, and traumas that exist with some poetry as well. Our job should not be to validate the feelings, stresses, or traumas found within the poetry, but to examine those elements because they are important to the cultures and times in which they were written. The goal, therefore, is not to attempt to establish PTSD within a poet, but to understand the manifestations of trauma response within the poem as articulated by a speaker who aims not only to speak from an individual perspective, but as a voice within a larger group. The speaker of the poem, of course, does not represent the culture, but she does allow for an insight in the articulation of stressors and trauma felt as a result of historical, and sometimes direct, trauma. Furthermore, some of the poets examined within this study wanted their work to be representative of their respective culture, especially when it is speaking to larger political imperatives that would break the cycles of trauma, especially as they discuss the disempowerment and poverty that many within their culture face, which reinforces the massive stressors with whom the people must engage. These massive stressors are not only related to disempowerment and poverty but are residual effects of historical traumas.

As has been stated, it is important to examine poetry in order to gain a greater insight into trauma because of the link poetry has to emotion and to history, thus providing a greater access to both individual and group pain. Poetry has the ability to give voice to memories that exist as images or that are not easily summed into words and are best articulated through formal devices such as metaphor or fragmentation. The articulation of historical trauma is partially because the direct victim of a traumatic event cannot always tell about their trauma and because trauma is often passed down from subsequent generations. Later generations discuss the trauma in order to work through, and ultimately gain control over, the trauma. Trauma has a unique grasp not only on the person directly involved in the traumatic event, but on the people of the group associated with larger traumatic events. For the individual directly impacted, they may attempt to escape the trauma and continue with their life without engaging with the emotions tied in with the trauma. This escape cannot be fully realized because of the flashbacks, nightmares, and repetitions that plague the victim long after the event; until the trauma is engaged and worked through, the event continues to haunt the victim. In a much similar vein, collective, traumatic histories of particular groups help to make up the identity of the group, thus individuals are tied to trauma, and unable to escape, because of being born into a certain culture. If the impact of this collective trauma has a pronounced influence on an individual, they must engage the trauma and attempt to work through the trauma in order to overcome the negative effects of historic trauma.

My study of the poetry of different cultures and races does not include Jewish literature; however, much of literary trauma theory has focused on post-Holocaust literature written by Jewish writers and much of that is pertinent to non-Jewish writers who work with traumatic events. Through my reading about literary trauma theory, I have noticed two common characteristics in post-Holocaust literature that point to the way Jewish writers express trauma within their writing. The first characteristic, the narrative of travel, is not unique to Jewish writers; in fact, I found the narrative of travel being used in Asian American, African American, Latino/a, and Native American writing, ultimately leading to a discovery of the fight-or-flight response that is inherent within the writing of these different cultures. What is significant, but not unique, about the travel narratives in the writing of Jewish writers is discussed in Anne Fuchs's *A Space of Anxiety: Dislocation and Abjection in Modern German-Jewish Literature*. Fuchs discusses the sense of travel by stating, "Migration, exile, and persecution all involve a loss of the connection with what one might call the 'space of homeliness,' commonly considered the locus of identity."[42] This type of travel is, of course, a reaction to the trauma associated with the Holocaust, but is also influenced by the Book of Exodus in the Bible. Fuchs differentiates the travel narratives by these post-Holocaust Jewish writers from travel narratives of the past by telling how they are not the "travel writings of the Enlightenment and Eurocentric kind where travel, with its pitfalls, dangers and challenges, acts as a positive catalyst, allowing the self to undergo a process of self-formation."[43] Instead, the speakers in the travel narrative of these texts are more representative of a "blinded maze-walker whose experience of the world remains disorientating and fragmented."[44] Coping with the diaspora associated with the Holocaust has caused a crisis not only with unhomeliness, but with identity.

A common thread in many of these poems, beyond the disoriented, fragmented, and aimless travel, is the quest to regain lost identity. Knight's poem "The Bones of My Father"[45] is a perfect example of this as the speaker is traveling in search for the bones of his father, which are representative of his identity. Such aimless travel, in the instance of Knight and other African American poetry, could also call upon the empowering nomadism of the blues singer, either indirectly or directly.

Searching for lost identity through travel is related to the idea of abjection and unhomeliness. Perhaps made most popular by Julia Kristeva in *Powers of Horror*, abjection is described by her as "what disturbs identity, system, order."[46] In her discussion, Fuchs describes abjection as "to be misplaced, astray and without identity. Abjection is a terrifying borderline state which estranges the individual from all social relations. It is the stigma of the modern subject that cannot locate itself via another object."[47] To be abject is to be othered and to be without identity, which, for Fuchs, is a direct result of the Holocaust. Identified and persecuted for being an other by the Nazis is an extreme form of trauma but is not unique to the Jewish people. The Holocaust, to be sure, was inconceivably horrific due to the industrialized form of mass destruction, which became even more devastating because "the Nazis killed or silenced most physical witnesses of the Holocaust but also because the bureaucratically administered genocide destroyed the ethical dimension of language, its capacity to forge bonds between human beings."[48] Jewish culture, however, is not the only culture to be subjected to genocide, thus abjection, the feeling of unhomeliness, and the wandering and isolation that are identified by these scholars as an effect of trauma are applicable to other cultures.

Because of the lack of homeliness, many of the poems dealing with trauma contain elements of travel regardless of the race of the poet. One such manifestation of travel occurs in the form of flight as part of the survival instinct. I have found, thus far, that there is not a specific trend of similar reactions that permeate one culture or ethnicity over another, which reinforces the idea that reactions to trauma tend to be somewhat universal. What is found, overwhelmingly, is the materialization of the survival instinct within the poetry that occurred as either fight or flight, although these take on different forms. In poems that exhibit flight, one can find examples of movement, often nomadic, in which the speaker, or other individuals within the poem, are attempting to flee. Although it may be an unconscious move for the speaker not to specifically tell or show that they are attempting to flee, it is apparent that they have a desire to get away from the current situation. In a similar vein of flight, the use of drugs, alcohol, or other opiates (a Marxist may include religion) allows for a temporary flight. The use of these substances can be an indicator that a trauma is either taking place, or has taken place, and the speaker is, or others within the poem are, attempting to leave the situation by any means necessary, even if the flight is not physical, but mental and/or emotional.

Often times, the flights occurring in the poems are due to not only incurred trauma, but also a result of unhomeliness resulting from diaspora and displacement. In some of the poetry of Japanese Americans and Native Americans, the unhomeliness is not only due to the change in the physical location, but separation from their native culture. Perhaps no greater component of a culture is the language of the people. As Japanese Americans, Native Americans, and other cultures become subjected to the oppressive, white, English-speaking culture, the ability to communicate with the oppressor resides within his language: English. In order to function in society, it is important to utilize the dominant language. To learn and use the dominant language is to become more at home in the dominant culture. One's mother tongue, just as the name implies, is usually where one feels most at home, thus having to speak the oppressor's language in order to communicate is to be, in itself, unhomed. However, in order to take the power back, some manipulate and distort the language in order to make it their own. The blues, we must remember, is premised on the bending of elements, both musically and linguistically, in order to create an art form distinct from that of the oppressor. We also find this as languages have evolved over time where words that traditionally meant one thing, such as the word bad, have been altered to fit a different culture and change the meaning of the word. Many such changes came from the jazz scene of the early 1900s.

As such, a second type of flight can be found in poetry where the speaker uses code-switching in order to empower the speakers of both languages rather than just speakers of English. Linguist Susan Gal discusses this type of activity by stating that code-switching is a form of "subversive reworking of dominant linguistic forms by subordinate groups: in short, the forging of new forms and identities out of the already symbolically weighted linguistic material at hand."[49] This type of flight is found in the poetry of American cultures where English is one of two or more languages spoken, such as within Asian American or Native American poetry. By interjecting words or phrases in Japanese, the speaker is able to take control from those who do not speak Japanese, which is many times the case with whites, and not only take power away but place the non-Japanese-speaking reader into an uncomfortable position of being outside a shared communality that the speakers of both languages share. By being able to communicate and share knowledge outside the reach of the oppressor, the poet is able to create a sense of empowerment within his audience that would only include those with the knowledge of the particular language, thereby inverting the power system. For example, Japanese Americans might be oppressed, yet they would have power over the oppressor by being able to communicate and comprehend one another outside the reach of the oppressor. In addition, by using one's mother tongue, the speaker or writer is able to carve out a place outside the reach of the dominant culture and establish a place reserved for the members of his or her culture.

As demonstrated, the narrative of travel is quite common in poetry that engages trauma, either directly or indirectly. The state of unhomeliness and abjection is commonly the result of the speaker engaging historical trauma. The common threads in many of the poems that engage trauma include, but are not limited to, disorientation, fragmentation, aimless travel, and the quest to regain lost identity. The quest to regain lost identity may take the form of travel in the form of abjection in which the speaker wanders rather aimlessly and blindly. However, travel that exists in these poems may also be a reaction to trauma and exist as a manifestation of the survival instinct. The incessant need to flee may take the form of physical movement or mental escape by means of mind-altering substances. A second type of flight may take the form of code-switching where the speaker may utilize her culture's mother tongue in order to carve a space for the people of her cultural heritage in an attempt to establish a space out of the grasp of the oppressor.

While flight within a poem can take many forms, the idea of fight is more direct and more easily found. In some instances, the poet's narrative is calling for a fight, as can easily be found in many poems of the Black Arts Movement. Other times, the call for fight resides in the speaker declaring him- or herself a warrior, as can be found in the poetry of Robin Coffee. Poets may also reference fighting or fight against the oppressor using methods unique to their culture, as we find in the poetry of Peter Blue Cloud. A final method to fight could be the use of language, images, or ideas that shock the reader. Profanity, violent images, or shocking statements force the reader out of his comfort zone, especially if the reader is white and reading a line that calls for the death of white people, which is found within many Black Arts Movement writings. By using these devices, the poet is able to present the trauma in a manner that mimics the reactions and memories of trauma and does so in an indirect manner. Therefore, by presenting the trauma in this manner, she may be able to generate connections with readers who empathize, thereby creating a connection with them that is not possible with people who have not experienced the same feelings.

Before closing, a final question I shall pose is "What purpose does a study like mine serve and how is it beneficial?" The obvious answer is that the use of literary trauma theory can demonstrate why the poetry of Nikki Giovanni or Amiri Baraka, written during the Black Arts Movement, was filled with so much anger, hostility, and violence, or why certain poems by Robin Coffee, Linda Hogan, and Mitsuye Yamada are filled with despair, confusion, and frustration. Obviously, the poetry from the Black Arts Movement was a call for change within society and for a radical reconstruction of social, economic, and social power, but we can gain a better understanding for the reason why this frustration existed and how it stems from more than one generation. The urge to fight or flee is the result of historical trauma, which has manifested itself for generation after generation, compounded with the potential for individual traumatic incidents that could have taken place and culminated into, for Baraka, fiery rhetoric that calls for the raping and killing of whites. An untrained reader may easily dismiss such poetry as being hate-filled, but someone who studies the poetry of the Black Arts Movement through the lens of literary trauma theory realizes that such language is used as a call for action after years of torture, abuse, genocide, and oppression. The same can be said for the despair, confusion, and frustration found within the poetry of Hogan,

Yamada, and Coffee. The historical remnants of torture, abuse, genocide, and oppression manifest within the poetry of these poets as frustration or despair rather than rage. Regardless of the emotion, examining poetry through a trauma lens allows for insights not available through other lenses.

Literary trauma theory and trauma poems also allow the reader to empathize with those who have either directly encountered trauma or may be linked to historical trauma due to their heritage. As we recall, poetry, more so than other types of writing, has a very strong connection to emotion. As Caruth and LaCapra have discussed, those coping with trauma often have a strong need to tell of their trauma in order to gain a greater understanding of it. Whether the trauma is direct or historical, many survivors have been said to feel isolated. By reading about the traumas of those who have endured similar struggles, survivors are able to develop a sense of community and are able to examine trauma from perspectives beyond their own. Writers and readers are able then to reinforce the idea that the traumas that have occurred are in the past and the future remains open to them. Moreover, poetry allows for a unique connection to trauma that is unlike other forms of writing because of its emphasis on poetic devices that are similar to traumatic memory. One such device that poetry is well known for is the use of imagery. Poetry, as has been discussed, lends itself more readily to expressing emotions and confessions. The combination of imagery and the tendency to express emotion can elicit and evoke feelings in readers, which can reinforce the sense of community. Ultimately, the reader is able to empathize with the speaker, especially if the reader has survived similar experiences expressed by the speaker of the poem.

In addition to the formation of community, literary trauma theory also allows readers to witness a version of history that is not always recorded in historical texts, and, what is more, literary trauma theory allows readers to have a greater understanding of the impact that trauma has had on people throughout history. Reading history may allow a single perspective on events that have taken place in our past, yet history is nearly always written through the voice and perspective of the oppressor and lacks the personal and individual stories of those who have been silenced. Rather than a cold telling of events that are found in historical documents, writers of traumatic narratives desire to evoke an emotional response from the reader and require a meditation on the form of communication.

Poems may not only present a narrative of a traumatic event such as a lynching or the voyage of a slave ship, but the poem may utilize various techniques, which may evoke anxiety in the reader beyond those that I have discussed so far. Poets may create short lines and stanzas to rush the reader through the poem or use enjambment to highlight certain words in order to heighten a sense of anxiety in the reading, thereby transposing a small bit of stress upon the reader. Other poets, such as Amiri Baraka, may use words such as "fuck" and "masturbation" to create anxiety that was especially effective in the 1960s and 1970s when audiences were not as commonly exposed to this type of language in movies, music, books, and poetry readings. The fact that using language such as this could be viewed as illegal, due to the obscenity laws of the time, would have further compounded the anxiety that people within the audience might have felt. For certain individuals, these words may still provoke a feeling of uneasiness.

It is important to examine poetry to gain a greater insight into trauma because of the link poetry has to emotion, thus providing a greater access to pain. Poetry also allows for an insight into the very constructs of representational impasse that comprises trauma. Trauma is understood as that which cannot be represented due to the severity of its impact on the survivors. In essence, trauma is form. What is most intriguing about trauma as form resides in our inability to comprehend with our normal tools of consciousness and representation. However, poetry also has the ability to give voice to memories that exist as images or that are not easily summed into words and are best articulated through figurative language. Traumatic figurative language is the means with which many poets are able to articulate that which is by normal means unrepresentable. As Auerhahn and Laub discussed earlier, traumatic memories are often represented through screen memories (which can take the form of images in poetry) and traumatic metaphors (which can appear as traumatic figurative language in poems). In addition, poets may represent the feelings of abjection and unhomeliness in their poems by producing narratives that discuss travel, flight (either physical or mental), and/or isolation. While these are often feelings that people coping with trauma may endure, poetry not only discusses these types of feelings but also combats them at the same time by producing a sense of community with the reader.

The importance of having a community for those coping with trauma cannot be overstated, yet this is not the only reason for a poet to take trauma from the private to the public sphere. Many trauma theorists see the benefit of survivors having their words heard as a means of empowerment and coping. Roberta Culberson states, "To return fully to the self as socially defined, to establish a relationship again with the world, the survivor must tell what happened."[50] This relationship with the world is a portion of what is tourniqueted with the advent of abjection. Steele also speaks of the benefit of the survivor telling of their experience and the need a survivor has for a witness. Steele argues, "In order to turn trauma into survival, one needs a witness for the reconstruction. . . . The witness is so vitally important because trauma, which cuts connections between people, also cuts off the survivor's access to an internal witness."[51] The internal witness that Steele is referring to is what must be utilized to reexamine the trauma in order that the survivor can work through the event and the pain associated with the event.

Thus, poetry aids in the empowerment of both the writer and the audience. The writer is empowered by means of reexamining the events associated with the trauma and is therefore able to own the trauma and is thereby able to more easily work through and cope with the trauma. In addition, by discussing trauma, the writer is able to work against abjection by gaining witnesses to the traumatic event by making their thoughts and feelings public rather than private. By doing so, they are able to open themselves to a community, which can aid in their coping. For the audience, the empowerment is quite similar. By listening to or reading poetry about trauma, the audience members, if they are also coping with the trauma, are able to become part of a community of survivors by witnessing the fact that they are not alone in their struggles with trauma. The community can work together as they cope with the trauma and work to ensure that similar events that cause the trauma do not happen again in the future. As we continue on with the chapters of this study, we will examine how the writing empowers three distinct cultures of the United States and how the trauma has affected the speakers of the poems. Through many of the poems, the writers describe events with a sense of abjection and displacement from community, and the very land that they once called home.

In the next chapter, these poetic articulations of massive stressors come into play in the poetry of Japanese American writers. Each of the poets selected in the following chapter spent time in the internment camps during different time of their lives. Each of the poets uses different poetic articulations of massive stressors to engage with the massive stressor of actually being imprisoned within the internment camps. From the writing of Soga, which was recorded during his time spent incarcerated, to the poetry of Yamada and Inada, who discuss their experience after the fact, each of these writers uses poetic articulations of massive stressors to record the events, the distress associated with the events, and in the case of Inada to move people toward empowerment.

NOTES

1. Cleanth Brooks, *The Well Wrought Urn* (Orlando: Harcourt, 1975), 9.
2. Brooks, *The Well Wrought Urn*, 9.
3. Jose Bleger, *Symbiosis and Ambiguity*. Edited by John Churcher and Leopoldo Bleger. Translated by Susan Rogers, Leopoldo Bleger, and John Churcher (New York: Routledge, 2013), 247.
4. Lucia Jerg-Bretzke, Steffen Walter, Kerstin Limbrecht-Ecklundt, and Harald C. Traue. "Emotional Ambivalence and Post-Traumatic Stress Disorder (PTSD) in Soldiers during Military Operations." *Psycho-social Medicine* 10 (2013): Doc03.

5. Jerg-Bretzke et al., *Psycho-social Medicine*, Doc03.
6. Jerg-Bretzke et al., *Psycho-social Medicine*, Doc03.
7. Julia Kristeva, *Powers of Horror: An Essay on Abjection* (New York: Columbia University Press, 1982), 4.
8. Stef Craps, *Postcolonial Witnessing: Trauma Out of Bounds* (New York: Palgrave McMillan, 2015), 2.
9. Craps, *Postcolonial Witnessing*, 2.
10. Irene Visser, "Trauma and Power in Postcolonial Literary Studies," in *Contemporary Approaches in Liteary Trauma Theory*, edited by Michelle Balaev (New York: Palgrave McMillan, 2014), 108.
11. Visser, "Trauma and Power," 108.
12. Ann E. Kaplan, *Trauma Culture* (Piscataway: Rutgers University Press, 2005), 91–92.
13. Antonius C. G. M. Robben, and Marcelo M. Suarez-Orozco. "Management of Collective Trauma," in *Cultures under Siege: Collective Violence and Trauma*, edited by Marcelo M. Suarez Orozco and Antonius C. G. M. Robben (Cambridge: Cambridge University Press, 2000), 44.
14. Maria Yellow Horse Brave Heart, "The Historical Trauma Response among Natives and Its Relationship to Substance Abuse: A Lakota Illustration, " in *Healing and Mental Health for Native Americans: Speaking in Red*, edited by Ethan Nebelkopf and Mary Phillips (Lanham, MD: Altamira, 2004), 7.
15. Brave Heart, "Historical Trauma Response," 7.
16. Philip A. May, "Overview of Alcohol Abuse Epidemiology for American Indian Populations." *National Center for Biotechnological Information*, accessed November 16, 2018.
17. Brave Heart, "Historical Trauma Response," 7.
18. Brave Heart, "Historical Trauma Response," 7.
19. Walter Kalaidjian, *The Edge of Modernism: American Poetry and the Traumatic Past* (Baltimore: Johns Hopkins University Press, 2006), 26.
20. Cassie Premo Steele, *We Heal from Memory: Sexton, Lorde, Anzaldúa, and the Poetry of Witness* (New York: Palgrave, 2000), 3.
21. Steele, *We Heal from Memory*, 3.
22. Steele, *We Heal from Memory*, 3.
23. Luminita M. Dragulescu, "The Middle Passage and Race-Based Trauma," in *Trauma and Literature*, edited by J. Roger Kurtz (Cambridge: Cambridge University Press, 2018), 274.
24. Dragulescu, "The Middle Passage," 275.
25. Bilyana Vanyova Kostova, "'Time to Write Them Off'? Impossible Voices and the Problem of Representing Trauma in *The Virgin Suicides*," in *Trauma and Literature*, edited by J. Roger Kurtz (Cambridge: Cambridge University Press, 2018), 163.
26. Nanette Auerhahn and Dori Laub, "Intergenerational Memory of the Holocaust," in *International Handbook of Multigenerational Legacies of Trauma*, ed. Yael Danieli (New York: Plenum, 1998), 22.
27. Ibid., 25.

28. Ibid., 26.
29. Ibid.
30. Ibid., 29.
31. Yusef Komunyakaa, "Reflections," in *Copacetic* (Middletown: Wesleyan University Press, 1984), 7.
32. Yusef Komunyakaa, "Annabelle," in *Copacetic* (Middletown: Wesleyan University Press, 1984), 8.
33. Yusef Komunyakaa, "Family Tree," in *Copacetic* (Middletown: Wesleyan, University Press, 1984), 96–99.
34. Auerhahn and Laub, "Intergenerational Memory," 33.
35. Ibid.
36. Ibid., 33–34.
37. Ibid., 34–35.
38. Sylvia Plath, "Daddy," in *Poetry Foundation*. Accessed June 13, 2019.
39. Etheridge Knight. "Once on a Night in the Delta: A Report from Hell," in *The Essential Etheridge Knight* (Pittsburgh: University of Pittsburgh Press, 1986), 111.
40. Dorothy Stringer, *Not Even Past: Race, Historical Trauma, and Subjectivity in Faulkner, Larsen, and Van Vechten* (New York: Fordham University Press, 2010), 4.
41. Stringer, *Not Even Past*, 5.
42. Anne Fuchs, *A Space of Anxiety: Dislocation and Abjection in Modern German-Jewish Literature* (Atlanta: Rodopi, 1999), 1.
43. Fuchs, *A Space of Anxiety*, 1.
44. Fuchs, *A Space of Anxiety*, 1.
45. Etheridge Knight, "Bones of My Father," in *The Essential Etheridge Knight* (Pittsburgh: University of Pittsburgh Press, 1986), 40.
46. Julia Kristeva, *Powers of Horror*, 4.
47. Fuchs, *A Space of Anxiety*, 4.
48. Hatja Garloff, *Words from Abroad: Trauma and Displacement in Postwar German Jewish Writer* (Detroit: Wayne State University Press, 2005), 12–13.
49. Susan Gal, "Language and Political Economy," *Annual Review of Anthropology* 18 (1989): 358.
50. Roberta Culbertson, "Embodied Memory, Transcendence, and Telling: Recounting Trauma, Re-Establishing the Self Author(s)," *New Literary History* 26.1 (1995): 179.
51. Steele, *We Heal From Memory*, 83.

Chapter Two

INTRODUCTION

I did not learn that the United States erected concentration camps for Japanese Americans and Japanese people, who happened to be on American soil, until I was in college. Even when I did learn, it was not through a class. Many of the students whom I teach today are not well aware that this appalling history took place. When informed, they immediately bring up the "camps" used for "illegal aliens" that exist in some of the same states and offer the clichéd idea of learning and failing to learn from our history. We often fail to learn from our history, but what is more damning is our unwillingness to consider what such history does to the people and cultures involved.

As was discussed in the previous chapter, traumatic figurative language, abjection, and unhomeliness are characteristics often found in poetry discussing trauma. Although the presentation of these characteristics can be overt or subtle, their existence in a poem is beneficial for the writer, as is the need to tell and the need for community. As attention is turned to the poetry of specific cultures, it is important to keep these characteristics in mind, as well as the history of the specific culture, to gain a better understanding of the traumas that occurred. This will be paramount for the next chapters, each approaching a different culture. However, the Japanese poetry examined is unique because part of the poetry examined discusses both direct trauma as well as historic trauma. In this section, I shall examine the poetry of Japanese Americans that engage with the historical trauma and massive stressors created out of the internment camps. As such, we can gain an insight into the speakers' articulation of distress, as well as, when examining Inada's poetry, see how this engagement can lead to empowerment. Obviously, the traumatic events that have occurred within Japanese American and Asian American culture reside far outside the span of the internment camps; however, the poetry surrounding the internment camps is significant because these events surrounding the internment camps, as well as the internment camps themselves, exist as a highlighted and magnified event in the larger traumatic history of Asian American and Japanese American culture and literature.

Before delving into the writings produced within Japanese American cultures impacted by traumatizing events, it is important to take a few moments' pause to examine a portion of the history that influenced the culture and writers. Historical and cultural traumas live beyond their time of occurrence. Cultural trauma passes from one generation to the next and affects each person differently, if at all. For many, this trauma occurred as people began to immigrate to the United States. Although many groups who came to the United States did so for a better life, they often fled racism, violence, and poor living conditions and were often greeted by the same in the United States. Many people fail to realize that, just like Americans of African descent, many Asian-Americans were not considered, or even allowed to become, citizens. Gary Okihiro states in his text *Margins and Mainstream* that "three years after the Constitution was ratified, the first Congress met and restricted admission into the American community to 'free white persons' through the Naturalization Act of 1790."[1] It was not until 1870 that the act was ratified to include African Americans and, finally, "Chinese nationals in 1943,"[2] and "the racial criterion for citizenship was eliminated completely only in 1952, 162 years after the original delineation of the Republic's members, or, according to the Nationalization Act, the 'worthy part of mankind.'"[3] Given that even the governmental Nationalization Act did not recognize people of Asian ethnicity as a "worthy part of mankind" until 1943, when many Japanese and Japanese Americans residing in the United States at that time were placed in internment camps, it is evident that the racism, hate, and actions of the U.S. government created historical trauma for an immeasurable number of people.

Although racism existed against Japanese living on American soil prior to World War II, after the Japanese attack on Pearl Harbor, public sentiment became filled with more hatred, fear, and suspicion. Shortly after the attack, FBI agents began raiding homes of people they believed to be spies and people working for the Japanese military and government. The highly trained and extremely efficient agents performed raids which were "choreographed down to the very last detail through advanced rehearsals and machine-like efficiency."[4] These rehearsals and the efficiency of the raids were very important to Hoover and other Washington leaders in order to "minimize hysteria among the populace and keep the U.S. home front on the gentlemanly side of martial law."[5] The actions of these raids kept the white American public feeling somewhat safe, but, in turn, demoralized some Japanese Americans, such as Kenko Yamashita, an Issei and Buddhist minister in Southern California who stated, "I thought the FBI would come pick me up soon because of this [the raids]. So I put my belongings into a suitcase and I prepared to go at a moment's notice. . . . I was ready for it from the beginning. But they came on March 13, 1942. I was tired of waiting so long."[6] The swift, calculated raids were efficient, not only in incarcerating what were perceived as dangerous people, but also in dissuading those being captured, along with onlookers, from generating any type of resistance. Roxworthy states that the spectacle of these raids "rendered victims and bystanders alike as passive spectators, overawed and even mesmerized."[7] It is evident, in passages such as these, that Japanese and Japanese Americans were not only psychologically overwhelmed by the shock of such raids, but they were left in a helpless state of looming anticipation. Many, if not most Japanese and Japanese Americans, were silent and nonresistant in their incarceration. Even after their release, most internees remained silent about the events surrounding their incarceration. Scholars have surmised this silence and nonresistance were cultural responses of the Japanese tradition, yet Roxworthy suggests, "We interpret former internees' silence not as a culturally conditioned response to adversity but rather as the structural outgrowth of the particular trauma of this particular internment."[8] Trauma is not only identified through repetition but in silence. The importance of silence as a means of coping within non-Western cultures is discussed in Stef Craps's "Beyond Eurocentrism." In the article, Craps examines the novel *The Memory of Love* by Aminatta Forna (a daughter of a Sierra Leonean man), which is about the civil war in Sierra Leon. Craps discusses how "the novel suggests that local coping mechanisms may even trump popular Western ideas about trauma treatment by showing how silence plays a beneficial role in keeping trauma at bay. Silence is repeatedly put forward as a valid way of surviving the suffering inflicted by war."[9] The same can be said about many of the Japanese and Japanese American prisoners. Many survivors repeat the incident in flashbacks, nightmares, or reoccurring thoughts and in literature as repetition in the narrative or literary devices, such as images. Another characteristic of trauma, as discussed by Roxworthy, is silence. While silence could explain this reaction, the poets of this chapter utilize traumatic figurative language within their poems, as well as abjection, unhomeliness, and isolation.

As opposed to the African American and Native American writers examined in this study, the Japanese American writers in this study do not focus on empowerment as much as these other groups. The poetry of the African American and Native American writers worked to formulate group resistance to the oppressor, yet, curiously, the Japanese American poets did not have the same thrust for empowerment in their writing. Although the Japanese internment camps were a brutal facet of Japanese American traumatic history, they are a concentrated example for the larger tradition of disempowerment and oppression that Asian Americans faced. This animus was due to the propaganda perpetrated by law enforcement and government officials, as well as the media, at the time surrounding World War II. They were viewed as (potentially) an enemy of the nation, at that time. Japanese Americans were already being scrutinized at a microscopic level, thus any movement toward empowerment, even in creative writing, could spell disaster for that individual.

In addition to the raids by FBI agents, vile lambasts appearing in the newspapers fueled hatred. Such hatred ultimately resulted in the establishment of internment camps in February 1942, where, according to the National Parts Service Department of the Interior, more than 110,000 people, mostly of Japanese ancestry, two thirds of whom were U.S. citizens according to Roxworthy,[10] were moved many times in an evacuation-type atmosphere. Such was the beginning of the trauma that arose from the civilian and military handling of Japanese-Americans during World War II. This was by no means the beginning of racism or hatred against Asian Americans. However, the trauma that was experienced by Asian Americans at that time, especially Japanese Americans, was not only a result of being placed in internment type camps, but it was also fueled by the public mentality and reinforced racism that spilled out of the rhetoric of this era. The time some spent under extreme stress, waiting to be taken from their home, as well as those who were taken in such raids, created a great deal of stress, anxiety, and in some cases, trauma. Even if some did not live in constant paranoia and dread of an FBI raid, those taken to the camps faced horrific conditions once incarcerated, and, as demonstrated in the poetry of Keiho Soga, many were separated from family and loved ones.

POETRY FROM INSIDE THE CAMPS

The internment camps constructed before and during World War II forced many Japanese and Japanese Americans from their homes, placed them in camps, oftentimes with horrid conditions, and isolated many loved ones. The camps were erected in desolate locations and surrounded by barbed wire, spotlights, and, at times, overzealous armed guards.[11] "Most, if not all, of the sites were overcrowded and not really prepared for human habitation," Roger Daniels states, and to make matters worse, "toilets and bathing facilities were minimal."[12] As if these problems were not difficult enough, "improper sanitation in the makeshift mess kitchens caused mass outbreaks of diarrhea,"[13] making living conditions in the camps almost unbearable, especially when one considers how many of the camps were often converted facilities, like horseracing tracks where many lived in horse stalls, which completed the process of dehumanization. To make matters worse, the treatment and propaganda that surrounded the camps reinforced racist ideologies already existent in the United States.

The influence of trauma on the prisoners in the internment camp is captured in *Poets behind Barbed Wire* where the poetry of Keiho Soga, Taisamboku Mori, Sojin Takei, and Muin Ozaki is edited and translated by Jiro Nakano and Kay Nakano. The four poets wrote in the tanka form, which offers a terse, thirty-one syllable platform for the poets to present their emotional response to the conditions of living *in and during* the incarceration. This is not the Wordsworthian type of poetry that overly romanticized definition of nostalgic poetry would convey. This form is a direct and immediate reaction to the traumatic experiences, which allows the poets to articulate the pain associated with their ordeal. Thus, this is not art for art's sake, but poetry created because of the conscious or subconscious need to tell. The poems articulate distress, pain, and trauma that reside within a cultural legacy.

Japanese poetry has a long tradition of poetic form focusing on syllabic structure with the tanka being just one example. The significance of the tanka being used by prisoners resides in the legacy of the poem rather than the syllabic structure. The tanka was often used, as described by the Academy of American Poets, by lovers because of its small size and its ability for the poet to express emotion. "Like the sonnet, the tanka employs a turn, known as a pivotal image, which marks the transition from the examination of an image to the examination of the personal response."[14] The poem itself is symbolic for the speaker's life in that traumatic events usually mark an individual's life as a pivotal event and greatly alter how one understands one's life. Given the brevity of the poem, the fact that this pivotal image marks not only a turning point, but also an entire line of the five-line poem, suggests how significant the event is to the speaker when considering that the remainder of the poem represents the speaker's life. The small stature of the poem reinforces how big the trauma is in comparison to the speaker's overall life. The size of the poem is also relevant due to the poor living conditions of the camps and the lack of material the prisoners may have had to write. Because of the scarcity of resources, such as paper and writing utensils, and because of the tanka's legacy of expressing emotion, this type of poem was appropriate for prisoners to tell of their emotions and frustrations. Furthermore, the pivotal image within the poem is as important as the emotional telling, given the connection to the manner in which images register within a survivor's mind in relation to trauma. Each of these aspects is important for the examination of poetry through a traumatic lens, but the tanka's use of both make it incredibly important for this study when considering the circumstances of when the poems were written.

ABJECTION, ISOLATION, AND UNHOMELINESS IN SOGA'S POETRY

Although some articles have discussed the life of Keiho Soga, there are no articles published in the past ten years, or before, examining his poetry. Little has been written about him, yet his poetry allows a great insight into the Japanese American internment experience and the trauma inherent therein. By beginning with Soga, we can follow the progression as the poetry written about trauma begins with the direct trauma incurred by Soga, to the poetry of Inada and Yamada, who experienced the internment camps in their youth and write about their trauma as historically manifested. In the poetry of Yamada and Inada, there are many more instances of traumatic figurative language, while it is absent from the poetry of Soga. However, many of Soga's poems contain references or traces of abjection, isolation, unhomeliness, and ambivalence, which allow the reader into a world created by the poet's experience and can provide an insight into the emotional reaction of the speaker and perhaps even the poet, although this study does not wish to examine the author, only the speaker. Many of Soga's poems lack a title; therefore, like the speaker, these poems lack a name or identity, thus reinforcing the isolation represented within the poem.

In Soga's poem beginning "There is nothing,"[15] the emotion and word of the captive being held during the war is presented to the reader. The poem, like many of the poems written by Soga, contains tropes of abjection, unhomeliness, and isolation. Soga is able to show the reader the immense pain associated with being separated from loved ones due to war. However, the most evident reason for pain in war, the death and destruction of humanity, remains unsaid. Thus, just as trauma is unrepresentable, the poem leaves the reasons for pain absent from the poem. Instead, we are given a perspective that focuses on the isolation that is the result of confinement. Given that the tanka was historically used by lovers to express their emotion, the isolation expressed in this poem is more significant because of the couples, families, and friends who were separated when incarcerated. Rather than a specific person, the audience for this tanka is no one and everyone, and it expresses the pain in a manner such that it remains largely unsaid and provides only an observation, thereby allowing his personal pain to remain unrepresented. Silence, as was discussed earlier, is a significant aspect of the Japanese internment as well as the response, or more appropriately, lack of a response, by those incarcerated. By allowing the speaker's personal pain to remain unsaid, the speaker is showing that the pain he is feeling is unable to be represented in words. In addition, the poem is moving beyond the archetypal tanka subject matter in which lovers proclaim his or her feelings through an intimate connection. Instead, Soga's poem is attempting to recover what has been lost due to isolation from culture and family in the internment camps. To show the significance, a poem usually used to discuss what has been gained (a lover) in private, in a form usually reserved for couples, becomes a poem about loss of culture (something shared by many) in public. This inverting of the norm brings attention to cultural tradition, the very thing being lost by the forcing of Japanese and Japanese Americans into the camps, stripping them of their culture and family, but does so in a manner that would normally only be recognizable to people familiar with Japanese culture and the tanka form.

The poem begins with this singular line: "There is nothing," which presents a nihilistic tone of both isolation and hopelessness, thus forcing the reader to engage with these feelings. In its entirety, the poem reads:

> There is nothing
> More sorrowful than war.
> Here alone,
> All of life's sadness
> Is brought together. (lines 1–5)

The second line of the poem continues the phrase by discussing the sadness of war. When read together, the two lines are stating how nothing is sadder and distressing than war. However, when the second line is read alone, it tells the reader that the idea presented in the first line, which focuses on isolation and helplessness, is more distressing and sadder than the actual war. As such, the situation of the speaker is worse than the actual war that placed him into this circumstance. This paradox of meaning, whether the nihilistic feelings overwhelming the speaker or the idea that there is nothing sadder than war, creates a type of confusion to the meaning of the poem, especially when considering that it is a tanka and meant to discuss love. Using this form and focusing on a different (perhaps opposite) overwhelming emotion, reinforces the emotions felt by the speaker. The confusion which may be gained through the multiple meanings gained from just the first two lines allows the speaker to project the confusion that he may feel given his present circumstances.

The pivotal image of the poem is the speaker declaring, "Here alone," (line 3). By allowing this line to follow the previous two lines, the speaker is reinforcing the isolation presented in the first line. The idea is powerful given not only the context of the other lines and the meaning inherent with them, but these two words exist on a line of their own, reinforcing the feeling of isolation. While this may be evident to the reader, the line, which is focusing on the idea of isolation, contains a pair of words rather than just one. The same idea could have been presented to the reader in the singular word "alone," but the speaker purposely used more than one word and thereby indicates that he is not alone. Therefore, there are many people there with him who share these feelings of isolation, even though they are incarcerated together.

This is the embodiment of abjection as the speaker is without home, companionship, nor identity and is the center point of the poem. The speaker, therefore, finds himself, much like many other Japanese Americans and Japanese immigrants, in a situation where the results of war have isolated him from the rest of the world, and the coagulation of misery is compounded within the internment camps. The people in the camp are without a country and without an identity, but share many commonalities, especially the grief and trauma resulting from their treatment in this nation and the racism perpetrated against them. They face the abjection identified by Kristeva as "what disturbs identity, system, order."[16] They are also the embodiment of abjection, as described by Fuchs, "to be misplaced, astray and without identity. Abjection is a terrifying borderline state which estranges the individual from all social relations. It is the stigma of the modern subject that cannot locate itself via another object."[17] Furthermore, Soga dislocates the poem from its familiar space, that of the private sphere, and uses this poem reserved for private feelings to express isolation from that which is most public: culture. In doing so, the speaker has also located himself as dislocated from his culture through a medium unique to his culture.

The concluding lines of the poem, following "Here alone" (line 3), refute the idea of being alone. The fourth line discusses the sadness of life, which is anything but singular in a person's life. However, by placing it after line 3, the speaker is reinforcing the idea of the extreme sadness by feeling alone, thereby suggesting that it is worse than any sadness ever felt by the speaker before. The final line refers to the previous sadness and simply states how it has gathered together. As such, by gathering together, the line is not only referring to the sadness of the previous line, but is also discussing the idea that the prisoners were all gathered into once concentrated prison, where he is, and that the sadness of being both forced together while separated from his loved ones is a feeling that comprises all the sadness that one could feel. The idea of feeling alone but also of togetherness is an ambivalence that is prominent within a great deal of the poetry selected for this study.

A second poem by Soga, that expresses the feeling of abjection, is his poem that begins with the first line "Like a dog."[18] In its entirety, the poem reads:

> Like a dog
> I am commanded
> At a bayonet point.
> My heart is inflamed
> With burning anguish. (lines 1–5)

This poem focuses on the isolation that many felt in the camps as well as on the treatment of the prisoners. The speaker in this poem is able to capture the anguish of being dehumanized by an armed captor who commands one's every movement as presented in the pivotal image of the bayonet in line 3. The more significant aspect of the poem is the idea of abjection and dehumanization rather than violence. The dehumanization begins immediately when the speaker compares himself to a dog, "inu." The use of dog, in this instance, is not an example of traumatic figurative language because the comparison is not between two traumatic events. The speaker is comparing himself to a dog *during* a traumatic event, but in order for this to be an example of traumatic figurative language, the event would have to be compared to another traumatic event. Even though this is not a traumatic simile, the use of this symbol is very significant. The image of a dog is very loaded because inu was the term used by inmates for those individuals who were working with the American government. According to Daniels, "There was some violence [in the camps], most of it directed not against the authorities but against fellow Japanese Americans who, it was believed, were collaborating with the oppressive government. Such persons were usually called 'inu,' literally 'dog.'"[19] Because the speaker uses this word, it provokes a feeling of isolation beyond that of simply being a prisoner. The dehumanization was isolating enough, but it was also compounded by abjection from infighting. More painful is the fact that the prisoners were regarded as enemies by their own country, and the pain is exacerbated by being regarded as enemies by their own people, which is realized by the use of the word inu. The result of the anguish felt by the speaker is abjection. The speaker here perfectly exemplifies the definition to the point that he presents his othered state beyond the realm of humanity. Rather than fear, anger, or hostility, the speaker suffers from anguish, a word synonymous with agony, grief, and suffering. It is precisely the suffering of being dehumanized and tormented by a violent captor that resonates as a massive stressor within the speaker.

The speaker states that he is "commanded" in the second line, which is not only a harsh word, but for a poem that spans only five lines, this word stands out because of its location at the end of the second line, so nearly in the middle of the poem, and perhaps more so because this word is the largest word of the poem. The placement of the word at the end of the line places emphasis on it, and it also draws attention to the "bayonet point," which resides at the end of the next line. The violence of this line is reinforced by the description of the speaker's heart, which is said to be "inflamed" in line four and "burning [with] anguish" in line five. The presentation of physical pain and intimidation suggested through the bayonet and the emotional pain found within the heart of the speaker aids in demonstrating the fear and suffering found within the speaker as well as others within the camp. Furthermore, the truncated lines and small words create an anxiety by forcing the reader through the poem quickly.

Understanding the torment felt in this poem provides greater insight into the sorrow expressed in Soga's poem "There is nothing." The fifth line, "Here alone," resonates more clearly if we consider the statements from "Like a dog," and the anguish therein felt by a person suffering abjection from his incarceration and despair from being turned on by his own countrymen. Because "There is nothing" and "Like a dog" were written by the same person during the time of his incarceration, and because both poems speak of war, I would contend that the poems can be read across one another to gain a greater insight into the situation of being imprisoned in an internment camp during a time of war.

The poems by Soga in *Poets behind Barbed Wire* contain moments of abjection, isolation, and unhomeliness, but the use of traumatic figurative language is not generally used. I believe the main reason that these Japanese American poets do not use traumatic figurative language in their poetry is because, unlike the other poetry examined in this study, the Japanese American poets, here, were currently enduring the traumatic events firsthand rather than enduring the trauma through historical trauma or looking back on the trauma. As such, there has not been sufficient time elapsed between the event and the examination of the event that allows for the use of traumatic figurative language. I believe this to be a device most often used by poets to describe historic traumas, and for these poets, the time has not elapsed to allow them to be as prone to engage with the traumatic stressor in this manner. This is not always the case, as the next poem demonstrates. Most situations where traumatic figurative language is used describes historical trauma. However, this final poem does use a traumatic figure to address the trauma felt by the speaker. In the poem examined above, the speaker uses a metaphor in reference to the trauma, but the language used to describe the trauma (referring to himself as a dog) is not referring to a previous trauma. Although the word is charged, it is not referencing a previous trauma. In the next poem, the speaker discusses the trauma associated with being a prisoner within the camp, but unlike the previous two, the speaker focuses on the stressors being felt by another inmate rather than the stress felt directly by the speaker.

Like the previous two poems, the speaker in "A fellow prisoner"[20] is a prisoner in a wartime camp and is struggling with the stresses associated with such incarceration. The poem reads, in its entirety:

> A fellow prisoner
> Takes his life with poison.
> In the evening darkness,
> Streaks of black blood
> Stain the camp road. (lines 1–5)

By having the speaker present a kinship with the other prisoner in the first line, the death of the other prisoner in line two becomes more significant and impactful for the speaker. However, the fact that the prisoner died by his own hand "with poison" in line two makes the death more tragic, as it not only conjures the negative implications surrounding the person's death, but also presents the physical manifestation of trauma due to the extreme psychological damage as a result of the incarceration. Furthermore, the focus on the death of a fellow prisoner by means of poison in the first half of the poem is significant because the audience is not given any information about the other prisoner with the exception that he is a prisoner and committed suicide by means of poison. The namelessness of the prisoner who died is significant in that it could refer to any prisoner incarcerated there, demonstrating the dire conditions of the camp and the manner in which the prisoners are having their senses of self forced from them due to their imprisonment.

The third and central line of the poem draws together the psychological darkness and the darkness of the night. The word "evening" in line 3 has double meaning, just as "darkness" does, in that evening could refer to the end of life when read in conjunction with the first part of the poem. This end of life could refer to the person who died or the possibility that the speaker foresees his own death in the camp. However, the darkness could also refer to the "black blood / Stain[ing] the camp road" (lines 4–5). The likelihood of poison creating a death with a loss of blood is highly unlikely, so the blood takes on a different meaning where it becomes traumatic figurative language. By the blood being black, the color could suggest a type of dehumanization, but what is more striking is the sound created not only the first letters of the words, but the words themselves. This sound mimics the sound of a beating heart, which could be read as either the haunting echo of the dead prisoner or the collective heartbeat of hope that may exist in the camp. However, given the lack of hope within the poem, that is unlikely. As such, the onomatopoetic alliteration acts as a traumatic haunting that could foretell future suicides in the camp by other prisoners.

The black blood is analogous to the darkness of evening found in the previous line, but since it "Stain[s] the camp road" (line 5), it is placing the blame of the death on the camp. The reason this metaphor is traumatic figurative language and not just a simple metaphor resides in the fact that it is comparing the present trauma to a different trauma in order to discuss something the speaker believes to be unrepresentable. In order to attempt to convey the feelings generated by the trauma, the speaker is attempting to compare the present trauma with another type of trauma, one that has left the roads filled with blood. Furthermore, the fact that we know nothing about the prisoner allows him to represent all prisoners, thus metaphorically staining the camp as visual persecution, literally staining and inscribing the camp enforcers with guilt. Unlike historically specific imagery, like that of whips and ropes within African American poetry, the historical nonspecificity of the bloodstained road strengthens the sense of self by being distinctively ubiquitous in its representation. The means of death of the prisoner is notable because it was (1) by his or her own hand, and (2) by means of poison. The suicide is important to our reading because it implies that the death was directly a result of the stress and trauma incurred from the incarceration. Clearly, any stress or psychological distresses exhibited by the prisoners are results of their incarceration. What needs to be remembered is that, although traumas can be collective because they occurred to a group of people, the reactions to the traumas and the way they are engaged in the psyche are unique to the individual. Because of that, making broad assumptions in comparing traumas is not only inaccurate but also misguided. Traumatic figurative language does not compare traumatic events in this way, and in fact, traumatic figurative language is not utilized to determine which atrocity was more devastating; rather, they are used in order to gain a greater understanding of the traumas themselves.

Traumatic figurative language is able to present what is often considered unrepresentable by deferring representation to another trauma. If we accept that trauma cannot be represented, it is only through traumatic figurative language that trauma can be represented. This comparing of traumas is not meant to clarify one trauma as opposed to another. The comparisons work to deepen the confusion that exists within the trauma by comparing it with another, thereby intensifying the terror associated with the events that have occurred. In addition, the comparison of one traumatic event with another through the use of a traumatic figurative language establishes poetic continuity between events, both historical and traumatic, that would normally be considered completely unrelated.

Returning to the poem, the fact that the death was by means of poison connotes that the massive stressors produced from being held within the camp is also a poison that eats away at the individuals to the point that they would choose to die rather than exist in such circumstances. As demonstrated in "Like a dog," the stresses associated with abjection could place a prisoner into this type of suicidal mentality, especially when we consider the anguish from the poem and the sorrow and isolation contained within "There is nothing." Just as in the poem "There is nothing," we find a tool normally reserved for the private sphere of lovers being modified into a tool and message for the public sphere. This collapsing of spheres is not only important as the poem uses a normally private template for commentary on public events, the poem also takes the idea of stress and trauma, something which is individualized and highly personal, and presents it in a public form that allows countless readers to explore. The poem is presented in the transhistorical public sphere to comment, using a traditionally private method, due especially to the wounded public sphere damaged by internment camps. Trauma exists both very personally and publicly when occurring to a group. This trauma and massive stressors, when internalized, has the ability to isolate individuals even though the feelings may be universal. Discussing the private feelings in a public manner enables the survivor to gain control over massive stressors and trauma by externalizing these feelings.

The reason the poetry written by Soga exhibits very few examples of traumatic figurative language is because trauma is presently occurring to the writer rather than as a type of historical trauma being reexamined by the writer. Not only is the trauma direct for the poet, but it is continuing to occur as Soga is writing his poetry. Traumatic figurative language is part of traumatic memory, and thus the poem is generated during a time of trauma rather than because of attempting to remember and sort through trauma. In both instances, many elements remain unrepresentable, yet it is through traumatic memories that traumatic figurative language is formed. In the next section, I will examine the poetry of Mitsuye Yamada, and like Soga, the poems contain elements of abjection, isolation, and unhomeliness, but traumatic figurative language is not overtly present. Although Yamada is producing these poems about the internment camps from memory rather than experience as Soga does, she does not utilize traumatic figurative language as one might expect.

ABJECTION, ISOLATION, AND UNHOMELINESS IN MITSUYE YAMADA'S POETRY

In the following section, the poetry of Mitsuye Yamada will be examined from her book *Camp Notes and Other Poems*, published in 1976. Yamada was chosen for this study because she, like Soga, spent time in the internment camps and writes about this time in her poetry. Unlike Soga, however,

Yamada spent time in the camps when she was a child, and she did not compose these poems while incarcerated, and thus more traumatic figurative language is used. I have found that poetry written about historical trauma, or poetry written about trauma years after the trauma occurred, tends to use more traumatic figurative language. This may be due in part because the trauma has had more time to be internalized, either through one person or generations. Traumatic figurative language is only one characteristic found within Yamada's poetry. As she looks back upon her past, it is evident that abjection was evoked because of her time in the Japanese internment camps, yet unlike Soga, the abjection is examined and articulated after incarceration.

Yamada was also selected due to the demonstration of ambivalence within a great deal of the poems within *Camp Notes and Other Poems*. Although a few articles exist examining Mitsuye Yamada's poetry, very little has been written about her poetry in the last ten years. Frederick C. Corey and Catherine T. Motoyama's "Toward Cultural Awareness through the Performance of Literary Texts"[21] does make note of Yamada's poetry in their 1989 article but focuses on the presentation of her poetry by a performance company; but it yielded little in regard to a close reading of her poetry. However, an article that is quite pertinent is Anita Haya Patterson's article "Resistance to Images of the Internment: Mitsuye Yamada's *Camp Poems*."[22] In her article, Patterson notes the ambivalence that exists, not only in the poems, but in the photographs that exist in the collection. Patterson focuses on the idea of obligation in Yamada's poetry, and she notes "One aspect of Yamada's poetics that has great significance for her poetry as a whole, is her profound ambivalence with respect to creative practice of making and arranging images. The critique of the image Yamada undertakes in *Camp Notes* reveals the central importance of obligation—and, more specifically, of situations and settings that involve obedience and disobedience—for her imaginative work."[23] It is this struggle with obedience and disobedience that cuts across many of Yamada's poems, which represent the psychological struggle that the speaker, and many people in the internment camps, faced.

In Yamada's poem "The Question of Loyalty,"[24] the speaker discusses the idea of signing loyalty papers, which Japanese prisoners were forced to do, to forswear any allegiance to the Japanese Emperor. As outlined in the poem, many prisoners, in order to be released from the prison camps, were forced to sign such papers, although not all did, in which case they were refused release. As a result, as one might imagine, this poem contains an overarching engagement with ambivalence.

Before even reading the first lines of the poem, the poem's shape on the page is of interest to the overall meaning. Although most lines are short, midway through the second stanza, the lines are indented to signify a quotation of the speaker's mother. On the page, along with the layout of the other lines of the poem, this creates a rough silhouette of a pregnant woman's profile. The three stanzas signify three portions of the body: the head, the body, and the feet:

> I met the deadline
> for alien registration
> once before
> was numbered fingerprinted
> and ordered not to travel
> without permit
>
> But alien still they said I must
> forswear allegiance to the emperor.
> for me that was easy
> I didn't even know him
> but my mother who did cried out
>   If I sign this
>   What will I be?
>   I am doubly loyal
>   to my American children
>   also to my own people.
>   How can double mean nothing?
>   I wish no one to lose this war.
>   Everyone does.
>
> I was poor
> at math.
> I signed
> My only ticket out. (lines 1–23)

In the first stanza, the speaker discusses how she registered as an "alien" (line 2) before. The first line of the poem ends with the word "deadline," which, when one considers the temporal context of the poem, creates an ominous feel. The use of the word "alien" in the second line furthers the ominous feel but also works to dehumanize the speaker and her mother, as well as all other Japanese and Japanese Americans. The idea of dehumanization is reinforced in the fourth line as the speaker is "numbered." In the first stanza, the speaker understands that she needs to register with the government and must not travel without a permit. The ideas are clear, and it appears that these ideas even make sense to the speaker. In fact, in line 3, she mentions that is not the first time that she has had to meet these kinds of deadlines.

    The lack of punctuation, outside of a few periods, does not create any confusion in the first stanza; however, the lack of punctuation in the second stanza (like a comma in the first line of the second stanza, as well as the lack of capitalization after a period in the same stanza) force the reader to slow down and reread lines for clarity. The second stanza, which makes the shape of the body, represents the emotion and confusion felt by the mother. Whereas the first stanza was logical, the ideas of forswearing allegiance to the Japanese Emperor is not as simple for the speaker's mother. The ideas of the mother, presented by an indented portion of the stanza, begin with her questioning what she will be considered in lines 12 and 13. More significantly, she discusses the trouble of trying to be loyal to both her children, who are considered American, and to her ancestors in lines 14 through 16. This emotional conundrum, represented as the pregnant belly on the page of the poem, suggests that not only is the question of loyalty a pregnant question, but one that impacts both her children and herself. It is also one that may be logical for the speaker, but the psychological impact that it has on the mother is much more significant.

The speaker of this poem states that she has no problem forswearing allegiance because she does not know the Emperor, yet the mother of the speaker protests and stresses how difficult it is to be from Japan and an American (lines 12–19). Like the speakers in previous poems I have discussed, the mother of the speaker in this poem is having great difficulty belonging to one or either group. Although the speaker has no trouble because he has little knowledge of or about the Japanese Emperor, and forswearing allegiance has very little impact on his psyche, the mother is forced to choose allegiance between the country that she now resides and the one of her birth. This poem demonstrates the struggle that many prisoners had as they tried to maneuver the difficulties of abjection and unhomeliness. Furthermore, if the mother forswears allegiance, this will be the birth of disloyalty of which she will carry the burden. The child will not carry this burden because she has no direct connection to the Emperor. However, the reader is given pause to the idea of allegiance to the Emperor as the word emperor is not capitalized in the second line of the second stanza. The lack of capitalization could represent a type of disrespect; however, I would suggest that this lack of capitalization is more relevant to the Japanese language, whose various writing systems have no capitalization, with the exception of the Romanized system. As such, the speaker is actually demonstrating ambivalence, much like the mother, except that she is being disloyal in a very enigmatic manner.

The persona of the mother is important as she represents place as well as culture within the poem. By using the figure of mother, the poem is able to show the difficulties many people could have had by having to sign allegiance papers against the country where some may have been born and others maintain cultural and familial ties. The mother in this poem represents not only Japan but Japanese culture, and, for some, family. Although many signed papers forswearing allegiance, they were not welcomed as, nor able to become, American citizens. Not surprisingly, many faced the feeling of unhomeliness, just as can be seen in Yamada's poem. In this instance, as was apparent in the previous poems, the unhomeliness stems from Japanese Americans and Japanese citizens residing in the United States being forced from their homes and placed in the internment camps. This poem engages this idea and is able to demonstrate the generational difference in thinking, which many prisoners had, and the senselessness of the imprisonment of more than one hundred thousand Japanese and Japanese Americans during this time.

Being forced to choose between the nation of one's ancestors and the country where the family now calls home and has (or in some cases, has not because barred legally) acquired citizenship, places a unique distress on a family unit to the extent that it inevitably endures a type of defeat, especially when the family, by nature of its ethnicity or original nationality, is regarded as an enemy in its new home. Having to sign away one's allegiance to the Emperor means having to forswear allegiance to one's cultural and ancestral home, and, in part, one's culture. While allegiances to the Emperor, or even Japan, may have not been an issue for most, it also meant swearing allegiance to the country that has decided to imprison those singled out as enemies. The result, regardless of whether the documents are signed or not, is abjection. In the end, as the speaker's mother states, no one wins the war. These lines, however, have double meaning in that everyone loses the war and that everyone wishes no one to lose the war. This double meaning is especially significant because of the double consciousness that those of the camp were forced to endure. Similar to W. E. B. Dubois's concept of "double consciousness," many Japanese Americans, both inside and outside the camps, were forced to endure an identity that could never be fully "American" because of their ethnicity and never "Japanese" because of their nationality or residence.

The final stanza is not only the shortest, but it contains the shortest lines. Whereas the first stanza represents the head and logic, and the second stanza represents the body and emotion, the third stanza represents feet and trauma. The small feet are reminiscent of foot binding, which was a traumatic procedure performed on women. It is well established that foot binding was a common practice in China. However, after the First Sino-Japanese War, foot binding was outlawed by the newly established Japanese government.[25] As such, Japanese influence over people of another nation outlawed and forbade a cultural practice, yet the Chinese culture remains strong. As such, just as the American government attempts to strip parts of the Japanese culture away from Japanese immigrants, the culture will remain strong. Hope glimmers in this idea, yet just as the foot binding could be seen as debilitating and negative to a segment of the population, maintaining allegiance to an emperor may have also been detrimental to the Japanese underclasses. However, this was not the first attempt at changing the culture of foot binding, as the influence of the Western ideals, especially through Christian missionaries, began to permeate China after the 1842 Opium War.[26] As such, this holds an ambivalent tone; although the practice was banned by the Japanese, it was also attacked by Western influence. Therefore, we see perseverance over Western influence in order to keep a tradition, but we also see the culture remaining strong after the elimination of the tradition. This ambivalence should not be surprising. In this last stanza, which does comprise the feet of the pregnant woman shape, the speaker gives four short lines that demonstrate that she is being stripped of her cultural heritage but also presents the finality of the decision through regret and hope. The speaker admits to signing "my only ticket out" (line 23) and proclaims she did so because she was "poor / at math" (lines 20–21). We can gather from this statement that, unlike her mother, the double identity of having ties to both sides did not mean a great deal as she refers to it as nothing (line 17). Rather than worrying about any kind of allegiance or historical ties, the reader chooses her freedom, a choice, which, in retrospect it seems, is somewhat regrettable. This regret is evident as the speaker freely states that she was "poor / at math" (lines 20–21) indicating that the decision she made may not have been the best. This reference to being poor at math is also a repudiation of the stereotype of the Asian who is good at math, thus disavowing the idea that all Japanese will be loyal to the Emperor or Japan. By disarming the stereotype of the Asian who is good at math, the speaker is attempting to reject all stereotypes that existed about the Japanese people and culture. Given the fact that, unlike his mother, the speaker quite easily traded her historical allegiances for her freedom, the decision apparently still haunts her mind as she speaks of it in the poem. "The Question of Loyalty" is a question that is beyond the speaker's control, and as can be seen in poems and history, the people of Japanese ethnicity can pledge their loyalty to the United States, yet white society's distrust endures regardless of what the individual in question says. To be loyal, therefore, is to be white, something that no one can change and something that one cannot become.

    The ambivalence in the poem is more pronounced by the mother, who is unsure, not only whether she should forswear allegiance to the Emperor but exists in the confusion of what she is becoming. The speaker also struggles with ambivalence, but she struggles in a less apparent way which is demonstrated both in the lack of capitalization of the word emperor and in a reference to the Japanese written languages that have no capitalization. The second occurrence of ambivalence occurs in the final stanza of the poem. As discussed, the feet of the poem harken to foot binding, which is not a traditional Japanese custom. However, just as the Americans are working to strip away the culture and loyalty of the Japanese and Japanese Americans, so did the Japanese work to strip away cultural aspects and Chinese influence upon the people of Taiwan. As such, there is a historically significant event that reflects upon the colonization of Taiwan by Japan just as there is the colonialization of the Americans over the Japanese. However, this idea of colonizing could also be reference to the manner in which the Western ideals colonized parts of China and fought against foot binding just at the Japanese did in Taiwan. Thus, the reflection of foot binding could refer to the Japanese as former perpetrators of colonialization or as victims in this instance as the Americans, and other Westerners, continue to colonize various Asian countries. Either way, the trauma of being forced to abandoned one's family and ancestors resonates in both histories.

As has been stated, by turning one's back on his or her ancestors, which the signing of this document represents, and by being always already disloyal because of one's race, the individuals of the poem face a dilemma with their identity and must face abjection. Japanese Americans in this poem are forced into this state of abjection and isolation from the nation in which they now reside and from the nation of their heritage. The result of their abjection becomes apparent in the next poem by Yamada. Not only does Yamada's poem "Cincinnati"[27] discuss the abjection and racism, but it utilizes figurative language, but not traumatic figurative language, in order to demonstrate the pain felt by actions taken against the speaker.

In "Cincinnati," the speaker is anxious to spend time in a new city where no one knows her until she is verbally assaulted and comes to the realization that she will be recognized as the enemy no matter where she goes. Like the previous poem, the topic of this Yamada poem is the idea of not being accepted because of looking like the enemy. The first line of the poem sets the initial mood of the poem as it begins with the word freedom: "Freedom at last" (1). The first portion of the poem contains an uplifting feeling and contains another significant word at the end of the second line, aimless: "in this town aimless / I walked against the rush / hour traffic" (2–4). The freedom held within the aimless wandering that the speaker does presents the antithesis of the incarceration of the previous poem examined and within many of the poems contained within the collection. This poem was placed in the section of her book that focuses on internment camps. In that context, we may deduce the speaker is discussing her freedom from incarceration. This is reaffirmed in the next two lines where the speaker states, "My first day / in a real city" (lines 5–6). Aimless also presents her as not being targeted, which is foreshadowing to what is to come within the rest of the poem. It is significant that the speaker feels and expresses these ideas within the beginning of the poem where she discusses her new freedom in a new city where she is not known by anyone: "where // no one knew me" (line 7–8).

The second stanza, comprised of only one line (line 8), focuses on the fact that no one knew who she was, which is a very ambivalent line. There is a positive aspect to no one knowing who she is given that the speaker has most likely left an internment camp where she knew many of the people. More importantly, by no one knowing who she was, no one would ridicule her for being placed in an internment camp nor would they consider her an enemy of the state. She would be able to have freedom in many aspects of her life, which is a refreshing change from her incarceration. However, the idea that no one knows who she is leaves her without friends or family to associate with or provide a safety net. She is now completely alone without, and is now isolated from, anyone she has ever known. This is a precarious and intimidating situation to be placed in, especially during this era. Further ambivalence exists as the line stands alone between a stanza discussing the joy of freedom and the attack she suffers. Although it is a bridge between freedom and attack, the line's meaning contains a stratified semantic quality that cannot mean only one idea.

In the third stanza, the speaker's joy of freedom is destroyed by the verbal assault of someone she passes and the spit that lands upon her face. The verbal assault comes from a "hissing voice" (line 10) followed immediately by an ethnic slur: "No one except one / hissing voice that said / dirty jap" (lines 9–11). The idea of the voice hissing does not align with the sound of line 11, thus the word hiss is used by the speaker to suggest something about the one who said these words. Given that the words are damaging and painful, it would not be a stretch to suggest that this could allude to a snake with the words and spit equating to venom.

The spittle physically and mentally stains the speaker and marks her with a sign of otherness. This is a physical and emotional mark, which exists as an assault of trauma upon her face:

> warm spittle on my right check.
> I turned and faced
> the shop window
> and my spittled face
> spilled onto a hill
> of books.
> Words on display. (lines 12–18)

This point is underscored by the reflection of "words on display" (line 18). The speaker is on display as an other. Like the books that are visible in the window the speaker passes ("words on display" (line 18)), so is the spittle of the assailant that came to rest on the face of the speaker. The line breaks of this stanza emphasize some of the most negative elements of the event by placing the most negative words at the beginning of the lines. By placing "dirty jap" (line 11) on its own, the phrase is emphasized or put on display, so to speak, making the phrase resonate even more strongly with the reader. As we move to the next line, the word warm (line 12), which usually does not have a negative connation, does in this instance because it is referring to the spit of the attacker. In lines 12 and 15, Yamada deemphasizes spittle by placing it in the middle of the lines. Thus, the word order and line breaks convey that the verbal insult holds more impact than the spit. In fact, the spit appears to affect her very little. The negative aspect is what the spit represents: the residue of racism.

These words on display, both in the form of the books the reader sees through the window and the spit that is on the speaker's face, are not communicating, as words typically do, but they are simply on display. There is a disconnection in regard to the functions of words in this stanza. The speaker can see the books, yet she is separated from them by the very glass where she sees her reflection. These books are little more than a collection of words that are unavailable to her because of the glass and what she sees in the glass. In her reflection, she sees the result of the ethnic slur in spit that runs down her face. In this instance, the words do not communicate, but they leave a visible sign of their utterance on her face. The speaker is marked by the words just as she is marked as an other by being of Japanese ancestry. As the speaker sees spit on her face by looking at the glass where she sees the other words on display, she is unable to find the words she needs in order to articulate the pain she feels from the verbal assault.

The fourth stanza discusses Cincinnati's Government Square, which has been the main transit exchange at the time as well as the home of many government buildings. The significance of Government Square is twofold. The fact that it was a center for transit reinforces the idea that the speaker, who is newly arrived in Cincinnati, is feeling unwelcomed and the need to move on because she is always already viewed as the enemy. This is reinforced as she describes the people moving in that area, as if they were parts of the spokes of some giant wheel reemphasizing movement:

> In Government Square
> people criss-crossed
> the street
> like the spokes of
> a giant wheel. (lines 19–23)

Secondly, the fact that this is an area comprised mainly of government buildings reminds the speaker and the reader that she was an enemy not only of the people who saw her, but of the government. Although she may have just left a government incarceration facility, she is in many ways always incarcerated by the very government that had declared war on her relatives. For her, there is no freedom and no escape.

The short, fifth stanza begins with the speaker attempting to raise her right hand, as if she were being sworn in to either court, but most likely as if she were declaring allegiance or citizenship, "I lifted my right hand / but it would not obey me" (lines 24–25). This hand, she states, would not "obey" (line 25) her; therefore, she is unable to raise her hand, thus rendering her unable to declare allegiance or citizenship. She is unable to do so because, in part, she will not be accepted as such. In the final two lines of the stanza, she states that her left hand is reaching for her handkerchief, "My other hand fumbled / for a hankie" (lines 26–27). This becomes incredibly significant after further reading, as the handkerchief is symbolic of her familial and cultural heritage. This inability to raise her hand while attempting to hold her right hand up signifies that the allegiance she is attempting to declare is related to her own culture. She is without a culture as neither will accept her, and she is unable to declare allegiance to either because she is forever unhomed.

In the sixth stanza, the impact of the assailant's words is quickly apparent as the speaker begins to weep as a result of the assault, "My tears would not / wash it. They stopped / and parted" (lines 28–30). The reaction focuses on the words and what the spit represents in the sixth stanza where she discusses how her crying would not wipe the spit away or the words or feelings. In fact, the tears are said to have "parted" (line 30). As such, just as her family, and many families of Japanese and Japanese Americans, were helplessly divided by the government, her tears are not able to combat this invasion and are instead divided as they approach the spit. Therefore, pain and trauma associated with the assault are evident by the tears that are unable to wash away the harm inflicted by the assailant's words. The speaker continues showing her reaction to the assault by stating that, after she wiped the tears and spit away with a handkerchief her mother had ironed, she lets go of the handkerchief into the gutter with other trash:

> My hankie brushed
> the forked
> tears and spittle
> together.
> I edged toward the curb
> loosened my fisthold
> and the bleached laced

> mother-ironed hankie blossomed in
> the gutter atop teeth marked
> gum wads and heeled candy wrappers. (lines 31–40)

This assault not only destroys the pleasant feeling of freedom the speaker holds in her heart, but the assault also has changed her attitude toward familial identity as she lets go of the handkerchief (line 38), which she used to wipe away the spittle and tears, to the ground. This cultural heritage manifested as a handkerchief cannot wipe away the spittle and tears, instead it mixes them together (lines 31–34).

Patterson states in her article that the "speaker's act of discarding the mother-ironed hankie in 'Cincinnati' is an act of disobedience, an explicit disregard for her mother's whispering wishes, insofar as the gesture suggests that even vigilant maintenance of the most obedient of demeanors would not protect the daughter from spittle and racist monikers."[28] Although this may be the case, I see the actions and images in this stanza as a move beyond the disobedience of her mother. The handkerchief (cultural heritage) combines the spittle (assault and trauma) with the tears, but it cannot wipe the skin completely clean. The speaker then lets the handkerchief (cultural heritage) drop to the ground. Discarding this item, one that her mother took particular care of, demonstrates discarding a portion of her heritage into the abandoned and forgotten items used up by others, due in part because she uses this item to wipe away the assault. Furthermore, it isn't that the speaker simply dropped the handkerchief; she states that she relaxed her "fisthold" (line 36), which demonstrates that she is no longer willing to fight, for her clinched fists have loosened and she has let go of her culture. The gum and wrappers that are in the gutter where she dropped the handkerchief (lines 39–40) are also scarred items that have been discarded, similar to the handkerchief, yet these items, unlike the handkerchief, have been scarred by the users intentionally, while the handkerchief was tainted as a result of an assault and voluntarily discarded through a forced choice and, therefore, not a choice. Finally, it should be noted that the handkerchief is said to have "blossomed" (line 38) as it lands in the gutter, thereby representing something that was once beautiful, like flowers, but, like the wilted flowers, it has lost its value, even if it was given by a loved one.

The poem closes with a powerful line that exemplifies the difficulty that many minorities face, but especially Japanese Americans during this time: "Everyone knew me" (line 41). The solitary line is presented after being offset after several blank lines and is a response to line 8, when no one knew her as well as the incident where she is assaulted. The peace and happiness at the beginning of the poem, where the speaker believes that she is now free, not only from imprisonment, but also from hatred in a place where no one knows her, has turned to despair by the end. The speaker is resolved to the idea that she is forever marked by her face so that she is always already marked as other, or the enemy, by many of the people she encounters, no matter where she goes. She can never be free because of this.

What is of particular interest in Yamada's poems "Cincinnati" and "The Question of Loyalty" is that the narratives of each are not that far removed from actual events that occurred in Yamada's life. In Helen Jaskoski's interview with Yamada, we find that, in 1942, Yamada and her family were prisoners at the Minidoka War Relocation Center in Idaho.[29] Because Yamada and her brother renounced loyalty to the Emperor of Japan, they were allowed to leave the camp.[30] When she left the camp, she went to Cincinnati, as discussed in her interview with Jaskoski:

> My mother felt that there was no other alternative except for me to leave [the camp] when I did. Then, I was free to go almost anywhere: there was a whole country to go to. I went to Cincinnati, where I got kicked out of a room I was renting in a sorority house. Apparently the alumni association of the sorority became very upset that there was a Japanese woman living in the dormitory.[31]

Although we must be careful not to deduce these similarities to be actual events, it would not be a stretch to believe that events similar to the ones described in the poems did happen to many Japanese Americans at this time. These descriptions could easily be biographical, yet we should be careful not to treat them as such. By writing them, externalizing her traumatic thoughts through words, Yamada gives her trauma external validation and political potential. Such is the power of writing. This is the approach that one must take when approaching poetry from a trauma perspective. Readers must be mindful of the poet, noting that the experiences written about may or may not be personal experiences, but the reactions and feelings of the speaker are valid because, in most cases, the events written about, such as those by Yamada, are events that may have actually occurred.

In her poetry, Yamada presents the difficulty many had living in the United States and the abjection, isolation, and unhomeliness that many faced. Unlike the poems of Soga, Yamada's poems discussed these feelings in speakers that lived outside the camps who still faced the racism and abjection, which was due in part to the internment camps. The hatred that many had for the Japanese and Japanese American people manifests in the sentiments and actions of people in Yamada's poem "Cincinnati." This hatred and racism existed before the twentieth century, but the rhetoric and actions of the government, politicians, officials, and the war itself created an atmosphere that did not frown upon, and in some instances encouraged, this type of behavior. The feelings, stresses, and traumas that Japanese Americans felt because of this atmosphere are evident in Yamada's poems presented here. In the next section, I will examine the poetry of Lawson Fusao Inada, which draws more from traumatic memory than the previous poems.

LAWSON FUSAO INADA, TRAUMATIC MEMORY, AND ABJECTION

Lawson Fusao Inada and his book *Legends of the Camp* provides a perspective that is somewhat different from Yamada's because Inada lived in the internment camps when he was only four years old, while Yamada was nineteen. Inada, unlike many poets, is able to draw off both direct and historical trauma because of the age he was when incarcerated. Some poems within *Legends from Camp*, such as the poem the book is named after, present images and narratives about the camps, but this poem was written with a disconnect; the speaker is distanced from the camp by discussing the events under the context of legends and describing them in retrospect rather than as presently occurring. The disconnect and distance taken by the speaker in "Legends from Camp"[32] is not unique to Inada's poetry. However, it should be noted that Inada does place the speaker in the first person, present in some of his poems about the internment camps, though the poem "Legends from Camp" is unique in its attempt to formulate legend. Legends are unverifiable histories and stories that are passed down through history. Although part of their history may be founded in actual events, legends are often the blending of facts and fictions, which are often exaggerated or changed with their retelling and with time. What is produced is a story of half-truth that has had to negotiate with the distance and disconnect from the actual event. The same can also be found in Inada's poem. The distance and disconnect found in this poem could be due to Inada's age when he was incarcerated and the fact that his understanding of the events in the camp were undoubtedly affected through the explanations of his parents and other family members who molded his memories and experiences. Because Inada was so young, the experience may have had a surreal feel, and thus is found in the repetition of "legend," an idea that surrounds some of the poems within the collection. This is precisely the way we should engage with the poem. Although the poet may have had a traumatic experience, the speaker exists as a blend of potential fact, but most likely fiction, which is one reason attempting to understand the poet through her poetry could be a folly. We must focus on the legend of the poem presented by the speaker.

Only a few articles examining the poetry of Lawson Fusao Inada have been written in the past ten years. Ryan Burt's "Interning America's Colonial

History: The Anthologies and Poetry of Lawson Fusao Inada"[33] focuses on resistance and the colonial policy of the American government. Although Ryan does make note of the double internment found in Inada's poetry (that of the indigenous internment and Japanese internment on the same land), the article makes little mention of trauma and focuses primarily on colonialization and resistance. Another article, Robert Grotjohn's "Remapping Internment: A Postcolonial Reading of Mitsuye Yamada, Lawson Fusao Inada, and Janice Mirikitani,"[34] examines both Inada's and Yamada's poetry, but, after a good deal of qualifying the idea of what postcolonial means and how it applies to the prisoners, the article focuses mainly on postcolonialism and the landscape in which the internees were held. The idea of trauma is never broached in this article. It is unfortunate that very little has been written about the trauma within Inada's poetry as it is quite evident.

Inada's long poem "Legends from Camp" contains twenty-five sections as well as a prologue. The speaker lists different facts associated with the incarceration of the Japanese Americans, but it concludes the prologue with two stanzas that harken back to the idea of the speaker's personal experiences, and those of others, that are so horrible they seem unbelievable, bordering on fiction (lines 54–61). The speaker of this poem openly suggests that these experiences, which may have been inspired by actual events, are altered by the passage of time, rendering the telling a mix between actual events and the subjective altering of memory. In addition, we can infer from these stanzas that the speaker is attempting to draw off his young memory, but the speaker recognizes that his memory and telling will ultimately be distorted by the passage of time and the impact of other stories that he has heard. This is important to note because the speaker recognizes that he is drawing on traumatic memories, and, consequently, his understanding of the actual events may be altered. Rather than examine every section of this long poem, I will discuss only those sections that are most pertinent to the study of trauma.

The third section of the poem is a short section that focuses on the fact that many Japanese Americans were taken into custody without protest. Believed by some to be a demonstration of commitment to the incarceration and willingness to be incarcerated, the speaker in this poem answers these ideas by stating that those who were arrested were hostages (line 77).

It is important to the concept of trauma to note how the speaker regarded the incarceration as a hostage situation rather than simply incarceration and indicates that any form of resistance might endanger the people already incarcerated. The distress associated with the uncertainty of loved ones being incarcerated is compounded by thoughts of the speaker's own potential or actual incarceration. It is clear the speaker is perhaps most concerned for the "elders" who were taken in the raids, as they are specifically mentioned in line 74 and are the only specific group mentioned in this section. The speaker is concerned for the elders not just because they are some of the most physically vulnerable, but also because they are the most revered in Japanese culture. The older members of their society being incarcerated in such a way is tremendously disrespectful. However, they are most tied to the traditional ways of Japanese culture, thus their mere existence is a manifestation of the cultural past, which is precisely what is under attack. As such, not only are people being held hostage, but so is the culture. The stressors are exacerbated by the fact that this is a terroristic hostage situation, not a state-run prison. There is a feeling of hopelessness, knowing that protests may have far worse consequences than a charge like resisting arrest. The fact that the speaker places the word "subversive" (line 75) in quotation marks indicates that he believes the arrests and incarcerations to be unjustified, yet the helplessness of the situation is magnified with the belief that they are reliant on the mercy and whims of their captors.

After being incarcerated, the lack of general necessities—such as freedom, adequate heating, lodging, food, safety, sanitary needs, as well as, in some cases, the ability to communicate and be with loved ones—dramatically impacts the stress of the individual and can ultimately lead to trauma. Section 4 follows the actions of a boy incarcerated within one of the internment camps. As this section of the poem begins, the speaker outlines all the things that have been taken away from the boy, as well as many other Japanese Americans. The fact that they were taken away increases the amount of stress on the incarcerated individuals because of the loss of resources and because they were not simply lost but were taken away by force. The poem is able to represent trauma by repeating the phrase "taken away" in several of the lines. This repetition is a constant reminder, and situation of consciously being aware, of being deprived and being lost without essential resources he was once used to possessing. In this section of the poem, the speaker provides a superb example of abjection as we see the boy who is now "misplaced, astray and without identity."[35] Everything, from his personal possessions and home to his very identity, has been stripped away from him with the exception of the knowledge that he now resides in the internment camp.

As the poem continues, the boy finds pleasure in following a truck that is spraying water on the ground. The boy is able to chase the truck and enjoy the water as a means of play. The boy temporarily forgets that he is incarcerated and finds pleasure when he can play. However, the boy eventually follows the truck to the point that he gets lost and is unable to find his way back to the barracks. This incident gives the boy his name. Like Lost Boy, many individuals within this poem are referred to, not by their given names, but by names acquired through incidents surrounding them. This demonstrates that possessions and freedom are not the only things lost. The very identity of a person is lost when Lost becomes his or her name; lost becomes who the person is. Like Lost Boy, the people in the poem reside in a state of abjection.

Much later in the poem, the speaker gives an insight into the camps, detailing more of the traumas associated in the camps. Section 19 of the poem begins by implying that, even though the poem to this point has spoken a great deal about legend, the fact was that there were other camps out there. In addition, this line portends that the lines to follow are most likely true. Thus, the inclusion of the word "legend" is not to take away any truthfulness or historical validity. The use of the word "legend" is part of the child's retrospection, and certainly it conveys how unbelievably horrible or traumatic these events were.

This section of the poem then takes a second turn in the next lines as the speaker admitted that no one knew what was happening at the other camps (lines 367–376). These lines force what follows back into legend because the speaker is telling us that all knowledge of other camps is speculative. This stanza demonstrates the frustration that people within the camps had trying to understand what was going on beyond the barbwire trappings where they found themselves living. Without good sources, or in some cases, any source, from which to gain knowledge, everything outside of the camp became legend. The difficulty that the people had understanding what was occurring in other camps, and perhaps more telling, the fact that they had a difficult time deciphering what occurred within their own camp, were not only because information was hard to come by, but because the events themselves were unrepresentable. The ability to communicate, about not only what has happened in a traumatic event, but the difficulty and inability to internalize the event, created a breakdown in attempts to directly articulate or represent traumatic events. As discussed in the next stanza of this section, the events are presented, but they are done so with a disconnection that refuses to identify the dead, and they show little to no emotion coinciding with the telling of events.

The second stanza of this section not only discusses the rumors that filtered in but also tells of the difficult conditions that prisoners faced within the camps, with people being shot and dying of heat and diseases (lines 370–374). As Daniels outlines earlier in this chapter, the sanitary conditions of the camps were usually very poor, and during insurrections, and sometimes even in everyday situations, prisoners were shot. To reiterate what Daniels stated about the overzealous guards, consider that there were "fatal riots at both California camps . . . in which armed soldiers guarding the camps shot unarmed protesters to death. And at a camp in Topaz, Utah, a guard killed an old man who, the guard claimed, had tried to go through the fence."[36] Referring to people as "so-and-so," as done in lines 371 and 372, has a hemisected effect on our understanding of events that take place. The first effect is the manner in which it reinforces the qualities of legend and rumor as the people are not named but referred to as "so-and-so." Talking about events that may or may not have occurred to people that are unnamed reinforces a phantasmatic quality to life in the internment camps. The inability to discern fact from rumor adds to the level of stress, both for the speaker in the poem and the people who resided in the camps. In addition, it is clear that the combination of the lack of personal safety from the guards, the lack of sanitation, the lack of medication, the lack of shelter from the heat, and as the speaker says "so little care," both meaning lack of care for the prisoners and lack of care to the conditions of the prisoners, it is more and more evident how these factors made the living conditions for the inmates traumatic. When we combine these factors with the lack of knowledge of events taking place in the world beyond the camp, which in some instances included the anxiety of not knowing the conditions of loved ones (yet another type of care), it is easier to see how they made for a trauma-generating environment for many prisoners.

The second effect resides in how the poet is able to demonstrate the idea of abjection in this portion of the poem by referring to people as "so-and-so" (lines 371 and 372). The people referred to as "so-and-so" are spoken of in passing, yet the reason they are spoken of is in reference to who has been shot and is either still alive or dead. Those who did not fall victim to violence but died of the heat or disease were also without identity and referred to only by infant or elder (line 373). The speaker uses these vague, impersonal words to describe the prisoners to underscore the dispassionate way they were treated. The guards shot them without hesitation because they, too, viewed the prisoners as nameless nobodies. By presenting these deaths in an aloof manner, the poem takes on a numb quality related, perhaps, to the prevalence of rumor and disinformation, as well as the impact of trauma. This type of numbing is quite common for victims of trauma, and the speaker, by using such a nonchalant and emotionally numb representation of the events, is able to present this characteristic of trauma in a successful manner.

Like Soga and Yamada, Inada's poetry contains examples of abjection, isolation, ambivalence, and unhomeliness. These, as we shall see through this entire project, are common themes in the poetry of different cultures. A second common element found cross-culturally in poetry engaging trauma is the use of traumatic figurative language. Figurative language is common in poetry, but traumatic figurative language is different from traditional figurative language. Traumatic figurative language is akin to traumatic metaphor as defined by Auerhahn and Laub.[37] In the following section, Inada's use of traumatic figurative language will be illustrated in two poems. The first is Inada's long poem "Legends from Camp," which will be followed by Inada's poem "Healing Gila." In both poems, the speaker is drawing connections to the reservations set aside for Native Americans and comparing them to the relocation camps used to incarcerate Japanese Americans.

TRAUMATIC FIGURATIVE LANGUAGE IN THE POETRY OF INADA

Many of Inada's poems discuss the internment camps that he and his relatives were forced to stay in during World War II. Abjection, isolation, ambivalence, and unhomeliness have been discussed with each of the poets of this chapter, yet while examining Inada's poems, there are several instances where the speakers of the poems utilize traumatic figurative language. Traumatic figurative language, as has been discussed, calls on other traumatic events in order to discuss what has occurred or is occurring to the speaker. Silvia Plath's poem "Daddy" is an easy example because in the poem the speaker discusses the abusive father and utilizes Nazi imagery and language to discuss the trauma that she feels. Of course, this is a very superficial examination of Plath's poem, but I use it here only to demonstrate what traumatic figurative language is and how it is used.

In Inada's poem "Legends from Camp," which has been examined in the previous section, there is a section that utilizes traumatic figurative language as a means to discuss the trauma and stressors incurred at the Japanese internment camps and compares the camps with the Native American reservations used to incarcerate Native Americans. Section 15, entitled "The Legend of the Full Moon over Amache," discusses how Amache, the camp the speaker is said to be staying in, was named after an Indian princess who died in the Sand Creek Massacre (line 297). By drawing upon the Sand Creek Massacre and discussing how it is believed that the Amache was named after an Indian princess, the speaker is able to create connections to the treatment of and atrocities committed against Native Americans and is able to compare them to the situation facing the Japanese Americans in the internment camp. The connection is reinforced as it is said that the princess's bones are said to have floated to where the camp is now, thus providing a metaphor of how the injustice, abuse, and trauma committed against Native Americans is now floating down through time to the Japanese Americans facing similar abuses. As trauma is often unrepresentable, it is sometimes necessary for survivors to utilize traumatic figurative language in order to articulate the abuse. This is one of the functions of using traumatic figurative language here.

The second function of using traumatic figurative language becomes apparent in the final two stanzas. The speaker refers to the full moon spoken of

Chapter Two

in the title and states that it is illuminating (lines 301–302), thus indicating that this metaphor is also being used to show the commonalities in treatment of Native Americans and Japanese Americans and their incarceration. Not only is this idea illuminating (line 303) to the speaker, but by understanding that the Japanese internment camp was named after an Indian princess (line 293) who died because of the whites' treatment of Native Americans in the past, it allows those in the camp the realization that they are not the first group to suffer this type of treatment. By bringing this idea to the forefront, the poem also allows this fact to be understood by people who are reading the poem and to better understand the repeated abuses that minorities have encountered at the hands of a racist government and people.

This idea is also presented in Inada's poem "Healing Gila,"[38] which refers to the Gila River Relocation Center, which was an internment camp for Japanese Americans during World War II. This camp is significant because it was placed on the Gila River Indian Reservation, so the land where this camp was placed is not only the place of trauma for many Japanese Americans but was for many Native Americans as well. The speaker is very careful, however, not to make any references to Native Americans in the poem. The fact that she is referring to Native Americans is inferred by the place and history she is discussing. In addition, she does not mention Japanese Americans in this poem. By not mentioning Native Americans or Japanese Americans specifically, she reinforces the idea that the trauma each culture faced is unrepresentable, and, because she strips their identity, she recognizes their abjection through allusion. The audience understands whom she is speaking about in both cases only because of the history of that place and the history of trauma associated with the place. The traumatic figurative language resides precisely in the comparison of the Japanese American treatment and the Native American treatment at the hands of the United States government. The traumatic figurative language in this poem exists, but it remains unsaid. It is precisely in the fact that it remains unsaid that it holds more power because it demonstrates the unrepresentativeness of trauma but also a form of solidarity that is able to cross cultural lines and the similar historical conditions that hold traumatic resonance.

The poem begins by acknowledging that people do not often discuss the fact that one of the Japanese internment camps was placed on the same land that was created for a Native America reservation, yet the reader does not learn what is being referenced until the second stanza. As such, the speaker begins by suggesting that we, the reader, should already know what people do not often talk about, thereby placing the reader in a position where we are forced to feel ignorant. This is purposeful because most people are ignorant to the event, yet they should be knowledgeable of this history. The second and third lines are nearly identical as the speaker plays with the phrase, "it goes without saying" (line 2) and replaces only the word "goes" with "stays." This minor change makes it apparent that the history of what has happened will not be impacted by discussing what has happened; after all, what happened will both "go" and "stay" without ever being discussed. This ambiguity is significant because the trauma of what has happened will remain whether we discuss it or not. If people would have discussed the treatment of Native Americans during the time of the Japanese internment, the events would have occurred regardless of what people said. Furthermore, this repeated action of created concentration camps is not something new for the United States, and this event was not the last time it occurred. As such, simply knowing our history and speaking of it won't stop the actions from occurring and repeating.

The speaker of the poem harkens to Native American trauma by using very loaded words in the second and third stanzas. The speaker highlights the words reservation (line 5) and contamination (line 7) by making them the last words of these stanzas. The term reservation helps identify the people being discussed, but it also calls upon the trauma of previous relocations performed by the white American society and the trauma associated with that type of relocation. Perhaps even more traumatic is how the contamination also refers to the intentional spreading of diseases, such as smallpox, to the Native American nations by the U.S. army in order to kill as many people as possible. The contamination of the poem refers to the two different races occupying the same space, both of which were placed there by the United States's government. The poem suggests that the Native Americans avoided the portion of the land that was taken (again) for the internment camp. Although the poem does not suggest that there could be a risk to health in regard to contamination, it can easily be understood that the contamination could refer to risk by association or avoidance from any of the Japanese Americans so as not to draw any unwanted attention from the government authorities.

The fourth stanza discusses the rundown nature of the camp, but the focus is on nails, pipes, and the foundations (lines 8–11). Nails and pipes are able to represent not only aspects of the camp, but they are also body parts. The nails are said to be "crusted" (line 9), which would be indicative of the squalor and neglect of the camp but also the inability for the prisoners to ever be physically clean at the camp, which has been discussed by Daniels. Moreover, being placed in such camps and enduring such treatment would also affect the psyche of the prisoners and sully their self-perception. The second body part mentioned, pipes (line 10), would refer to the more colloquial "wind pipes," which would aptly represent the chocking confines of the camp and the overwhelming psychological torment brought about by incarceration. Lastly, the stanza concludes by discussing how the foundations within the camp were "failing" (line 11). This refers to the manner in which the foundation set up by the Constitution is failing the people of Japanese ancestry, but, as mentioned in the poetry by Yamada, some prisoners and other Japanese Americans were turning away from their cultural heritage, out of necessity, ultimately creating a failing frustration of their identity.

The fifth and eighth stanzas are identical as they both ask, "What else is there to say" (lines 12, 21). Both lines follow a stanza that ends with ellipses, suggesting there is more to be spoken; however, these lines are also connected to the first stanza that discusses not speaking and the ideas of things going without saying. As such, these lines reinforce the idea that there is nothing more to say because the trauma and misery goes without saying to those within the camp, and with the damaging of pipes, perhaps nothing could be said, even if there was more to say. These single-line stanzas reside as two different turning points within the poem.

The first turning point moves the focus of the poem from the present conditions of the land and camp, which is overtly negative, to a more positive discussion of the land and the people who once occupied it. Stanza 6 focuses on the land and people who resided there and describes the land as "lush" (line 13) and the people who lived there as "gifted" (lines 14, 15) with "wisdom" (line 15). The stanza concludes by mentioning "irrigation" (line 16), which refers back to the pipes in line 10, but also sets up the main focus of stanza 7. In this stanza, the speaker discusses how the Native Americans set up canals throughout the area and worked with nature through "balances" (line 20) as opposed to how the Americans treat not only the land, but people. This discussion of the past also highlights the manner in which the prisoners are being held and treated in a manner that is not human or humane.

The second turn of the poem moves away from the positive history of the land and shows the transition repeating the phrase "then came" and showing how the region changed as each transition occurred. The first is "nation" (line 22), suggesting the arrival of the Europeans and the destruction to the land and people, which is apparent in that "death" is what comes in line 23. After death comes the "desert" in line 24 followed by "camp" in line 25. The fact that both the camp and desert occur after death is suggesting that the camp is both a fate worse than death as well as a type of hell, given its placement after death along with a dry, desolate area.

In stanza 10, the poem uses repetition again by repeating lines 2 and 3 in lines 27 and 28. The stanza begins with word play with the word desert, first using it as a noun and then adjective, suggesting that the desert is not without people. The repetition here is referring back to the first stanza and reminds the reader that, just because people are not talking about it, there are people being held prisoner in the desert. These stanzas, and their repetition, conclude by discussing how the new prisoners, the Japanese, are imprisoned on land that was once set aside for the Native Americans who faced the same fate. Both groups were relocated because of fear, and the fact that they were moved to the same location should not be lost on the reader.

The speaker is able to mingle the trauma of both cultures by discussing the destruction and trauma incurred by Native Americans. The speaker also mentions how the camps have now been erected upon land that was given to Native Americans in a similar situation where a group was displaced from its home and moved to a place specifically designed to hold it as a means to make whites feel safer. The speaker believes the parallels are rather apparent by stating, "It goes without saying" (lines 2, 27) in line 2 before discussing the camps being placed on the land set aside for Native American reservations, and the idea is expressed again in line 27 before mentioning the pain on line 29, suggesting the pain felt by one culture may be similar to the pain felt by another culture. In addition, the fact that "It stays without saying—" (line 28) follows both instances of "It goes without saying" (lines 2, 27) suggests that by not discussing the traumas incurred by the groups or the parallels, the pain and the camps, will not go away.

The final stanza of the poem, which is also the final line, simply lists four things: "wind, spirits, tumbleweeds, pain" (line 29). This line is one of the most meaningful in the poem in how it is able to articulate historical and cultural trauma without discussing it directly. Tumbleweeds, which is a term that describes a variety of different plants, are found primarily in the desert. As the plant reaches maturity, it dies and separates from the root system. It is through the tumbling motion, as perpetrated by the wind, that the plant, now dead, is able to have the seeds dislodged, and it is then able to reproduce but do so in a manner that allows the seeds to move a great distance. As such, it is the wind that not only moves but changes the tumbleweed, allowing it to reproduce and have a life after death, but only as it is affected by the wind. Much like the tumbleweed, the Japanese Americans have been uprooted (both from their original home of Japan, but also through the internment camps) and are, or will be, reproducing in a new location. Between these words are the other two words of the line, "pain" and "spirits," and they apply directly to those imprisoned. Whereas the wind moves and changes the tumbleweeds, the pain of the incarceration changes the spirits of those who are affected. Although there are many parallels with the tumbleweed and the Japanese Americans, the more resonate aspect of the line resides in the impact of the trauma and the manner in which it galvanized several generations of people, both Japanese Americans who lived through incarceration or were related to those incarcerated. Moreover, the stigmatizing and hateful actions and rhetoric perpetrated by the government were manifest and inculcated within the minds of many Americans who believed the stereotypes and hateful rhetoric about Japanese Americans. As such, the trauma and racism against Japanese Americans lived on much longer than the internment camps; thus the tumbleweed is also representative of trauma seeds of hate through time and space. Given that the poem is published in 1997, the speaker is most likely examining the aftereffects of the pain as it continues to affect people many years later. Therefore, the symbolism of the tumbleweed applies to both.

As the line is read, however, the words spirit and pain appear in the wrong order, until the poem is examined closer. The only other two single-line stanzas say the same phrase, "What else is there to say" (lines 12, 21). The number of the lines is significant in that the same two numbers are used but only in a mirrored reflection, just as the wording of the last line suggests. Furthermore, this line is answering the questions posed by these two stanzas and is telling a great deal that was not actually said in the poem.

The traumatic figurative language used by Inada in these poems forces the audience to recognize the similarities present in the treatment of Japanese Americans in internment camps and the treatment of Native Americans in the past. By doing so, the poems are able to compare the treatment and the trauma to horrors that people may have attempted to grasp before and represent the unrepresentable by means of deferring the representation of trauma. Trauma, which is said to be unrepresentable, is acknowledged by drawing the audience's attention to another unrepresentable trauma. Each event goes beyond fair representation, so a way to aid in the represented is by calling on another trauma. One trauma is not equal to the other, and it is not the purpose to decide which was more devastating or traumatic, but it is through, and perhaps only through, the discussing of multiple traumas and by comparing them that one may gain an understanding into that which cannot be represented.

More importantly, this poem is attempting to unite people across different cultures not only to recognize the similarities that exist in the traumatic histories of the culture but engage in a cross-cultural empowerment to dismantle the oppression that minority cultures face. The speaker in Inada's poem attempting to empower through engagement with trauma is unique for Japanese American poets discussed in this study. One of the main reasons, I would speculate, has to do with his age when he was incarcerated. Unlike Soga and Yamada, Inada was a child when incarcerated, thus his understanding of the situation would have been far different because of his age. More importantly, his engagement with the massive stressors is more akin to those engaging with historical trauma because he would have learned a great deal about the events from his community after the events. Unlike poems of the Black Arts Movement and American Indian Movement who try to unify the people of that specific culture in order to rebel against the oppressor through a single front, Inada's poem is looking to cross cultures in hopes that people of multiple cultures can see the oppression and inhumane treatment of people in order to promote resistance. The movement toward empowerment is key when attempting to break the cycles of massive stressors that continue to impoverish and disenfranchise people, which is often the result of traumatic pasts. Although the Native American poets and African American poets discussed include calls for empowerment in their writing, such a cross-cultural call for empowerment, which is this overt, is unique to Inada.

NOTES

1. Gary Okihiro, *Margins and Mainstream: Asians in American History and Culture* (Seattle: University of Washington Press, 1994), 6–7.

2. Okihiro, *Margins and Mainstream*, 7.

3. Okihiro, *Margins and Mainstream*, 7.

4. Emily Roxworthy, *The Spectacle of Japanese American Trauma: Racial Performativity and World War II* (Honolulu: University of Hawaii Press, 2008), 78.

5. Ibid., 78–79.

6. Ibid., 80.

7. Ibid., 82.

8. Ibid., 2.

9. Stef Craps, "Beyond Eurocentrism: Trauma Theory in the Global Age," in *The Future of Trauma Theory: Contemporary Literary and Cultural Criticism*, ed. by Gert Buelens, Sam Durrant, and Robert Eaglestone (New York: Routledge, 2014), 55.

10. Roxworthy, *The Spectacle of Japanese American Trauma*, 58.

11. Roger Daniels, *Prisoners without Trial: Japanese Americans in World War II* (New York: Hill, 1993), 63–65.

12. Daniels, *Prisoners without Trial*, 65.

13. Daniels, *Prisoners without Trial*, 66.

14. "Tanka: Poetic Form." *Academy of American Poets*. Last modified September 26, 2004. Accessed June 13, 2019.

15. Keiho Soga, "There is nothing," in *Poets behind Barbed Wire*, ed. and trans. Jiro Nakano and Kay Nakano (Honolulu: Bamboo Ridge, 1983), 21.

16. Julia Kristeva, *Power of Horror: An Essay on Abjection* (New York: Columbia University Press, 1982), 4.

17. Anne Fuchs, *A Space of Anxiety: Dislocation and Abjection in Modern German-Jewish Literature* (Atlanta: Rodopi, 1999), 4.

18. Keiho Soga, "Like a dog," in *Poets behind Barbed Wire*, ed. and trans. Jiro Nakano and Kay Nakano (Honolulu: Bamboo Ridge, 1983), 19.

19. Daniels, *Prisoners without Trial*, 63.

20. Keiho Soga, "A fellow prisoner," in *Poets behind Barbed Wire*, ed. and trans. Jiro Nakano and Kay Nakano (Honolulu: Bamboo Ridge, 1983), 57.

21. Frederick C. Corey and Catherine T. Motoyama, "Toward Cultural Awareness through the Performance of Literary Texts," *MELUS* 16, no. 4 (1989): 75–86.

22. Anita Haya Patterson, "Resistance to Images of the Internment: Mitsuye Yamada's *Camp Notes*," *MELUS* 23, no. 3 (1998): 103–27.

23. Patterson, "Resistance to Images," 105.

24. Mitsuye Yamada, "The Question of Loyalty," in *Camp Notes and Other Poems* (Berkeley: Shameless Hussy, 1976), 39.

25. Melissa J. Brown and Marcus W. Feldman, "Sociocultural Epistasis and Cultural Exaptation in Footbinding, Marriage Form, and Religious Practices in the Early 20th-Century Taiwan." *PNAS*. December 29, 2009. Accessed June 13, 2019.

26. Alison R. Drucker, "The Influence of Western Women on the Anti-Footbinding Movement 1840–1911." *Historical Reflections/Réflexions Historiques* 8, no. 3 (1981): 179–99.

27. Mitsuye Yamada, "Cincinnati," in *Camp Notes and Other Poems* (Berkeley: Shameless Hussy, 1976), 42–43.

28. Patterson, "Resistance to Images," 124.

29. Helen Jaskoski and Mitsuye Yamada, "A *MELUS* Interview: Mitsuye Yamada," *MELUS* 15, no. 1 (1988): 97.

30. Jaskoski and Yamada, "A *MELUS* Interview," 107.

31. Jaskoski and Yamada, "A *MELUS* Interview," 107.

32. Lawson Fusao Inada, "Legends from Camp," in *Legends from Camp* (Minneapolis: Coffee House, 1993), 7–25.

33. Ryan Burt, "Interning America's Colonial History: The Anthologies and Poetry of Lawson Fusao Inada," *MELUS* 35, no. 3 (2010): 105–30.

34. Robert Grotjohn, "Remapping Internment: A Postcolonial Reading of Mitsuye Yamada, Lawson Fusao Inada, and Janice Mirikitani," *Western American Literature* 38, no. 3 (2003): 246–70.

35. Fuchs, *A Space of Anxiety*, 4.

36. Daniels, *Prisoners without Trial*, 64.

37. Nanette Auerhahn and Dori Laub, "Intergenerational Memory of the Holocaust," in *International Handbook of Multigenerational Legacies of Trauma*, ed. Yael Danieli (New York: Plenum, 1998), 33.

38. Lawson Fusao Inada, "Healing Gila," in *Drawing the Line* (Minneapolis: Coffee House, 1997), 110–11.

Chapter Three

INTRODUCTION

The following chapter will engage with poetry produced around the Black Arts Movement and is highly significant to this study in the way it engages traumas, by using poetic articulations of massive stressors, to empower African Americans. Trauma is often (but not always) historical rather than direct in African American poetry. Unlike the poems examined in Japanese American poetry, African American poetry is focused more on traumatic figurative language, in part because, in some instances, more time has passed and allowed for more reengagements with the events and their historic pasts. Additionally, the poets are documenting traumas that may not have directly impacted them. It is understood that the initial traumatic experience occurred when the first slave ships began transporting African slaves to North America. Furthermore, not only are the remnants of that historical trauma still present in African America, but the countless occurrences of attacks, both physical and psychological, after slavery have left traumatic scars just as well. As a result of the attacks and legacy of trauma that exists within African America, the Black Power Movement and the Black Arts Movement arose in the mid-twentieth century to empower African Americans from the oppression felt as a result of treatment stemming from slavery and Jim Crow. The poets of this chapter are writing just before and during this period, when the empowerment of African Americans was a key issue, not only politically, but in the arts. The poems are working to establish a community of artists sharing similar experiences and people who have lived through and fought in the struggle to give voice to African America.

The focus of this chapter is on two poets of the Black Arts Movement because it is in this time that we find a group struggling to find a voice and aesthetic outside of the dominant white culture. Just as trauma attempts to represent the unrepresentable, writers of the Black Arts Movement attempted to represent that black experience in the United States in a manner that was removed from the culture that existed at that time. Therefore, the Black Arts Movement had to articulate an experience, and one intrinsically tied to trauma, not connected to the Eurocentric model of art and expression. The writings of such as Amiri Baraka worked to carve out a space for the articulation of the black experience, but also to push against white oppression in a manner that unapologetically denounces the idea of white superiority. These writings not only articulate trauma inherent within the culture but attack the white culture by projecting negativity and refusing readability to a white gaze. The traumas spoken of in the poems of this chapter, and in the Black Arts Movement, harken to the events of slavery when people were attacked physically and psychologically, yet through those events, a culture emerge based on both trauma and resilience. Many of the poems also engage with the lynching as well as Jim Crow laws that permeated the United States, especially in the South.

The African American poems examined in this study were selected, like the Japanese American poets, because of their level of engagement with traumatic events of the past and discussion of massive stressors. Obviously, many African American poets engage with this type of subject matter, like Larry Neal, Haki Madhubuti, Gwendolyn Brooks, and Yusef Komunyakaa, to give a very small list. However, the poets of this study were selected because of their involvement with the Black Arts Movement, their obvious level of engagement with trauma, but also the manner in which they attempted to empower their audience by discussing and engaging these traumas.

Although many traumas occurred to many African Americans during the twentieth century, it was in the traumas incurred during American slavery that was the genesis of African America. One of the most damaging aspects of American slavery for African slaves was the attempted obliteration of culture, not only by the process of enslavement itself, but by forcing people of different African cultures together in the New World. The stripping away of one's native culture combined with the well-documented horrors of slavery created irreversible destruction to past cultural identity. Ron Eyerman discusses these events, stating, "As opposed to psychological or physical trauma, which involves a wound and experience of great emotional anguish by an individual, cultural trauma refers to a loss of identity and meaning, a tear in the social fabric, affecting a group of people that has achieved some degree of cohesion."[1] What these events caused, instead, is the formation of a new cultural identity, and in turn, a collective memory that took generations to form. Eyerman discusses this reformation of identity stating, "Slavery formed the root of an emergent collective identity through an equally emergent collective memory, one that signified and distinguished a race, a people, or a community depending on the level of abstraction and point of view being put forward."[2] This identity, although formed through the traumatic events of slavery, continued to be molded through the freeing of the American slaves, the racist laws that promoted segregation and propagated lynching and eventually lead to the creation of a new identity through forced assimilation.

In the writings of the Black Arts Movement, a greater push emerges for African American culture to refuse to be subjugated by Eurocentric standards. The Black Arts Movement worked fervently against the white standard of art and, by creating a relationship between art and politics, worked toward an independent culture and nationhood. Larry Neal, in his essay "The Black Arts Movement," discusses this relationship; he states of the Black Arts Movement that "it envisions an art that speaks directly to the needs and aspirations of Black America. In order to perform this task, the Black Arts Movement proposes a radical reordering of the western cultural aesthetic."[3] Other scholars like Hoyt W. Fuller discuss how "young writers of the black ghetto have set out in search of a black aesthetic, a system of isolating and evaluating the artistic works of black people which reflect the special character and imperatives of black experience."[4] Writers needed to move away from what was valued through the white perspective and establish a system of aesthetic values focused on the black experience, exemplifying what it meant to be black in America and glorifying the experience. Furthermore, Hoyt continues by discussing how the Organization of Black American Culture worked "toward a definition of a black aesthetic… [and were] deliberately striving to invest with work with distinctive styles and rhythms and colors of the ghetto, with those peculiar qualities which, for example, characterized the music of John Coltrane or a Charlie Parker or a Ray Charles."[5] Many poets, like Gwendolyn Brooks, Amiri Baraka, Larry Neal, and Haki Madhubuti did precisely this. The Black Arts Movement worked to give an authentic voice to the black experience in America, something that writers like Baraka promoted and succeeded in doing.

In an essay written two years before Neal's, LeRoi Jones (Amiri Baraka) discusses this need for an African American literature that gave voice to the uniqueness of the experience and culture. Jones states:

> A Negro literature, to be a legitimate product of the Negro experience in America, must get at that experience in exactly the terms America has proposed for it, in its most ruthless identity. Negro reaction to America is as deep a part of America as the root causes of that reaction, and it is impossible to accurately describe that reaction in terms of the American middle class; because for them, the

Negro never really existed, never been glimpsed in anything even approaching the complete reality of his humanity. The Negro writer has to go from where he actually is, completely outside of that conscious white myopia. That the Negro does exist is the point, and as an element of American culture he is completely misunderstood by Americans.[6]

It is evident here that Jones not only sees the need for the black experience to be articulated but also the need for the black community to cultivate that articulation around a distinctive African American culture. Furthermore, because it has been heavily affected by trauma, as Jones alludes to, the culture needs to tell of the traumatic experiences. Jones is desirous of an authentic black voice speaking of the black experience, and a great part of that experience, as can be seen in the above statement, is one that has evolved from centuries of trauma.

This trauma is, as Eyerman would stipulate, a cultural trauma. However, Eyerman's idea of cultural trauma falls short when we refer back to the ideas of Brave Heart and LaCapra. Historical trauma, as discussed by Brave Heart, attempts to occupy the space unfulfilled by the concept of post-traumatic stress disorder by examining how past atrocities can inform the future and manifest in subsequent generations. In poetry, these manifestations take the form of poetic devices such as abjection, isolation, ambivalence, unhomeliness, and traumatic figurative language.

Establishing a new aesthetic for African America was the encumbrance shared by many black artists of the 1960s, which was also to represent the unrepresentable. How does one articulate the pain, anger, anxiety, and sadness associated with the horrific abuse of a racist society resting upon the legacy of slavery? Many black writers of the Black Arts Movement had the task of representing an experience, which was considered invaluable by the dominant white culture, but had to forge new ground for aesthetic representation. African Americans had the tools in a well-established set of formal devices and genres that were specifically African American, like spirituals and the blues, but the task was to move this aesthetic forward and do so without the influence of white society. Writers of the Black Arts Movement, in the advancement of the black aesthetic, had to represent something that had not been represented to the extent they desired. There were poems by African Americans, but the goal, in part, was the creation of an entire movement of black arts, one that sought to overthrow the control of white America and to reside outside of white America's reach. In addition, the black experience is one filled with trauma, which, as we understand, is unrepresentable. Therefore, the task to be undertaken by black artists was twofold: the writers must represent an experience that cannot be represented aptly (trauma) and a new type of writing must be established that exists outside the control and influence of white America.

In order to understand this twofold purpose, it is beneficial to examine the work of Fred Moten. In his book *In the Break*, Moten wrestles with the idea of a type of suffering that renders the survivor mute. Moten's interest is in phenomenology, of which he states, "More specifically, I'm after the way concern with perception and cognition (of the things themselves) leads to the deconstruction of ontology."[7] Moten is describing the reaction to trauma as a person often being unable to articulate events that occur or completely comprehend them, but also as the way one's very being is deconstructed by the trauma. The experience is both one of tremendous horror, but also empowering. The event is so destructive that it renders one without the appropriate tools in order to comprehend or articulate what has been experienced, and the individual is thus left reevaluating their very own existence and the world around them. In the above statement, Moten is referring to Wittgenstein's idea of phenomenology, and continues by saying, "What I'm after depends upon thinking through the question of the relation between semiotics and phenomenology *by way of the phenomenon or experience of noticing an aspect . . . which is . . . the experience of meaning or of an insistent interpretation.*"[8] Furthermore, Moten states, "There is no phenomenology, only phenomenological problems—and to notice in passing that noticing an aspect—a phenomenological problem that, as we shall see, demands *description* in light of its exceeding of *explanation*—is in the aftermath or wake of this formation: not but of not but of not but of."[9] The description of a traumatic event is in a perpetual state of deferment where the survivor cannot aptly describe what has occurred, thus the description often takes the form of traumatic metaphor. Trauma, as we have seen and will continue to see, resides—much like the phenomenon described by Moten—in the rupture where an explanation exceeds, as he stated, the demand for description and makes clear the need for a new ontology. Moten continues by stating that "we must attempt a description of an experience whose provenance or emergence is not reducible to logical structure, pictorial internal relation, or internal similarity."[10] Trauma is precisely this type of entity: a specter of a phenomenon whose existence goes beyond fair representation but continues to haunt survivors and their ancestors. Moten continues to describe trauma phenomenology as "an experience of the passage or cut that cannot be explained because those formations upon which our explanations must be grounded . . . are themselves so profoundly without ground."[11] In order to compensate for this exact difficulty, poets who attempt to represent trauma utilize traumatic figurative language in order—through a type of phenomenological substitution—to compare, and in some situations, replace one traumatic event with another in hopes that the reader's familiarity with one or both of the phenomena will allow an understanding of the event and emotional reaction to the event, when neither are truly able to be represented.

Given that trauma is unrepresentable, African Americans not only have struggled with articulating the trauma that has permeated their culture's history and provided the very grounds for identity but have had to deal with the long legacy of racism that forbade literacy and promoted inequality in educational opportunities, creating barriers to those attempting to articulate the pain, anger, and struggle that resided in African Americans during and after slavery. Trauma, one must remember, has the ability to resound within a culture for numerous generations; thus, the abuse, rape, and torture American slaves experienced for hundreds of years would not simply cease after the last American slave died. Likewise, the animosity, cultural racism, superstructure of oppression, and hatred that existed in white America did not cease either. What is very apparent in African American culture is the fortitude of even those forbidden to become literate to create art outside the bounds of the written word. It was in song that a great deal of African American art was first recognized. It was also in song that African Americans attempted to represent the unrepresentable. It is no wonder then that poets, such as Baraka, become so dedicated to the study of African American music, as he did in his books *Blues People*,[12] *Black Music*,[13] and *The Music: Reflections on Jazz and Blues*.[14] Music has the ability to represent emotion without relying on words in order to do so; thus, it is not surprising that one can find places in the poetry of Baraka where he is using not only elements of song, but also utterances, transcribed to paper, where language fails him. These same utterances appear in poems about John Coltrane, most notably Sonia Sanchez's "a/Coltrane/poem" and Haki Madhubuti's "Don't Cry, Scream."

In this chapter, it is essential to consider the poetic devices that these poets used in order to represent historical traumas saturating the culture. The discussion begins with Amiri Baraka as he engages the problems affecting black America and gives voice to those. As Neal states, "Without a culture, Negroes are only a set of reactions to white people."[15] The key, to return to Moten's phenomenology of trauma, is that carving out a culture while being unhomed and abject—as those of the Black Arts Movement were attempting to do—is produced with relative ease given the many devices and genres invented by slaves in order to express the traumas they were encountering. Many of these modes of artistic expression, such as spirituals, the blues, and field hollers, were created to overcome situations where slaves, and later African Americans, were denied other means of articulation. Poets of the Black Arts Movement, such as Baraka, found it relatively hard to carve out a space for this culture given the adversity of the oppressive white aesthetic establishment that found no value in African American art that did not strive to be white. Baraka's poem refuses to conform to white expectations, and in many ways, his poem "Black Dada Nihilismus"[16] does just the opposite. "Black Dada Nihilismus" comes from his 1964 collection *The Dead Lecturer*, from what William J. Harris refers to as his transitional period between bohemianism and Black Nationalism.[17] The final Baraka poem, "Legacy,"[18] comes from *Black Magic*, Baraka's first collection from his Black Nationalist period. Each of these poems articulates the struggle with historical trauma within the speaker as well as the attempt to represent an unrepresentable phenomenon of trauma in order to define a new African American ontology, much akin to what has been discussed by Moten's examination of phenomenology. Clifton's poetry, like Baraka's poetry, also utilizes a variety of poetic devices found in poetry discussing historical trauma. In addition, Clifton also discusses the idea of working within an aesthetic value system that is uniquely black and that resides outside of the influence of whites. This is especially prevalent in her poem "my mama moved among the days,"[19] which calls upon historic trauma, but also the idea of building a community upon the workings of ancestors. It cannot be overlooked that the person of power in the poem is a woman, and it is through the woman's work of building community that empowerment is found. This suggests that it is through the help of strong women in African American culture that empowerment and strength can be found as well as the formation of community. Although it is well understood that writings of the Black Arts Movement desired to establish a community, both artistically and politically, that advanced black thoughts, what is less discussed is the idea that the very culture and history that the artists and writers of the Black Arts Movement are drawing from is one filled with trauma and discussions of how these thoughts have manifest within the poems. This chapter will engage with this often overlooked and rarely acknowledged facet of poetry of the Black Arts Movement and demonstrate how and where trauma is resonant within the poetry.

AMIRI BARAKA, TRAUMA, AND REPRESENTING THE UNREPRESENTABLE

Over the past ten years, there have been dozens of articles written about Amiri Baraka. Given his death in 2014, some have focused on his life and written in memorial thereof. Other scholars have focused on his poetry, like Kathy Lou Schultz who focuses on Baraka's poem "Wise, Why's, Y's" as a modern epic poem in her article "Amiri Baraka's 'Wise, Why's, Y's': Lineages of the Afro-Modernist Epic."[20] Jeffery St. Onge and Jennifer Moore focus on Baraka's poem "Black Art" as a form of rhetorical dissent in their article "Poetry as a Form of Dissent: John F. Kennedy, Amiri Baraka, and the Politics of Art in Rhetorical Democracy."[21] Ahmad Mehrvand, in the article "A Postcolonial Read of Amiri Baraka's 21st Century Political Poem on America,"[22] examines Baraka's controversial "Somebody Blew Up America" through a postcolonial lens, and does well to highlight the political aspects, both contemporary to the poem and historical, but the article could have been aided in a deeper understanding of trauma theory, especially given that the poem was composed in the shadow of one of the United States's most televised traumatic events. Finally, Ephraim Scott Sommers analyzes Baraka's poem "Black Art" in the article "The Poem of Anger: Amiri Baraka, Troy Dent, and Adrian C. Louis"[23] and focuses on the anger inherent within Baraka's poem, as well as the other poets listed in the title. Although the examination does highlight several instances in the poem where Baraka is able to express anger, this study would benefit by a more in-depth analysis through the trauma lens in order to decipher the meaning of the anger and emotion presented in the poem.

The various periods of Baraka as a writer are well documented. For this study, I chose two poems by Baraka: one poem from his "Transition Period" between 1963 and 1965, and one poem from early on in his "Black Nationalist Period" published in 1969. These poems were chosen, in part, because of the readiness with which they lend themselves to the literary trauma lens, but also because they represent a period in Baraka's life where he, much like African American literature, existed in a major transition, from the very beginning of the Black Arts Movement until its midpoint. It is in this transition and the grasping for identity that one can find a great deal of engagement with representing the unrepresentable in the form of poetry grappling with the discussion of historical trauma and establishing a voice. In this poem, Baraka is struggling to represent his identity and articulate trauma more so during his "Transitional Period." During this period, Baraka was working to establish his voice. Later, as Baraka became more involved with Black Nationalism, he found a community that had similar ideas to fight the oppression that African Americans faced. In Baraka's poem "Black Dada Nihilismus," his speaker attacks the white society as he works to establish a representation of Blackness outside of white cultural standards. Later, in Baraka's poem "Legacy," the speaker focuses more on the impact of historical trauma as it has negatively affected African American society. The focus of "Legacy" is less on fighting against the white oppressor but examining the destruction that history and historical trauma has left behind.

In Baraka's poem "Black Dada Nihilismus," the speaker attempts to describe the struggle of articulating the black experience while fighting against the oppressive white culture that has permeated the lives of African Americans. Black writers faced the daunting task of articulating an experience that was uniquely African American while using the language and Eurocentric ideas intrinsic to the United States. In order to call attention to the difficulty of expressing the black experience by using a white language, the speaker calls upon aesthetic values of Europe by naming artists (Mondrian) and cultural movements of Europe (Dadaism and De Stijl), that broke outside of the cultural norm in order to express their art and experience. However, by referencing Dadaism and artists like Mondrian, the speaker has selected forms that are nonrepresentational while rejecting the prevailing standards of their time, especially when considering the historic traumas these artists confronted, such as World War I and global revolutions against bourgeois nationalism. The idea is further articulated by the use of the word "nihilismus," which is not only a word created by the speaker—thus rejecting the prevailing standard of English and mimicking a Latinate sound and look—but also calls upon the idea of nihilism. When broken apart, the word becomes "nihilism us," calling on blacks to reject the established laws and institutions set up by the white society. By mixing two words, dada and nihilismus, which both call on the rejections of prevailing standards, with the word "Black," the speaker is calling on African Americans to do exactly this for a new kind of representation. This means, of course, to be black is to be in a state of abjection. This idea becomes further complicated as one understands that the black experience is one filled with direct and historical trauma, and is, in itself, unrepresentable. This abjection is not just a representation of a culture victimized by the dominant white superstructure but is a means of attacking white culture. The speaker in the poem is continuing on in the African American tradition of projecting vehement negativity toward the dominant white culture. These types of attacks exist within many of African American arts, from the blues, to spirituals, slave hollers, and the writings of Langston Hughes and Claude McKay.

The ambivalence created by attempting to produce discourse about the black experience while fighting against the oppressive white culture and being shackled to the oppressor's language is not unique to this poem. The speaker must either use a language not his own, which resides outside the oppressor's, or use the language of the oppressor while trying to create a space uniquely African American, which is always already tainted by European culture. The language of African America is English, so turning to another language is not an option. The third option is to say nothing at all. Therefore, in this poem, in particular, this struggle resonates both in content and ambivalence. The struggle to express this conundrum in the oppressor's language or say nothing at all is best expressed in the first line of the poem that begins with a period.

This conundrum is also articulated in Patrick Roney's article "The Paradox of Experience: Black Art and Black Idiom in the Work of Amiri Baraka." Roney examines "Black Dada Nihilismus" and other Baraka poems in how they test the limits of "the various American modernist reincarnations of identity."[24] Although Roney does well to analyze Baraka's works in this manner, his critique could be better understood through the aid of literary trauma theory. Roney is right to begin his critique of Baraka's poem by focusing on the blank space and period that begins the poem. Of it he says:

> This suggests more than just a rhythmic delay in the breath. It also complicates the very beginning of the poem as an absolute beginning, rendering it indistinguishable from an ending. What is it that inhabits this space, separated from the text of the poem by a period? It is a silence *outside* the text, a language beyond language, yet just as surely does it indicate "pre-text" that is equally an "infra-text," the very text of the tradition and its Others, a tradition no longer governed by a law of identity, which is no longer *a* tradition. The poem marks itself off against this silent space in a gesture of opposition, yet it just as surely belongs to it: Destruction cannot simply do away with this space, it owes something to this silence; and the ensuing poem, which lies on the *other* side of the period, is already spoken by it even as it strives to make that silence speak in a denaturing idiom.[25]

Roney is absolutely correct in his assurance that this silence is "a language beyond language" because what is being articulated in this poem is the representation of something that is unrepresentable. Although Roney is more focused on a poststructural analysis, his reading is nuancing toward trauma. What is missing, amongst other things, is the focus on ambivalence. While Roney and I may agree on the silence at the beginning of the poem, to a degree, this is where our consensus ends.

By starting the poem with a mark used to indicate the end, the idea of ending this oppression is presented immediately but subtly. With such an unusual start, the reader is forced to struggle with this beginning that is marked as an ending. Furthermore, this paradox has perplexed publishers as well. In the 1991 publication of the poem in *The LeRoi Jones/Amiri Baraka* collection, no period exists in the beginning of the first line. However, in the 2014 *The Norton Anthology of African American Poetry*, volume 2, 3rd edition, as well as the 2015 publication of *S. O. S: Poems 1961–2013*, the period does exist. Further confusion is evident as the period is against the first letter of the first word, thus the period lacks the space before the word, and the period acts as if it were against the last word of a sentence, yet the first word of the sentence is capitalized. There is silence within this gap before the period, as Roney articulates, but it is the silence and inarticulation of trauma and the silence of knowing how to proceed.

As the poem begins, the speaker immediately begins calling for a contrast with the first line. The speaker is calling for the examination, indicated by the first line calling for a contrast and investigation of the prevailing standards. This is suggested by the title and the first three lines of the poem. Although the speaker is demanding an examination of that which is considered false, he is also referring to historical trauma by immediately calling upon people who have been killed, many of whom, it can be argued, did not meet the false standard discussed in line 2. This idea of trauma is extended in the next lines. Since the line break between lines 4 and 5 falls as it does, the murder perpetrated in line 4 is directed at those who have performed ethnic cleansing, but the attempt is one that is weak in comparison to the power of his God. The speaker then brings forth a "him" who is to be one of the people responsible for ethnic cleansing rather than God, given the first letter is lowercase. The speaker then indicates that the ethnic cleanser will not be forgiven for his actions (lines 6–8). Yet, this last line is highly significant when examined against line 9 where the speaker restates the title of the poem (lines 8–9). As has been discussed, the dada nihilismus is calling for a rejection of prevailing racist standards and values, yet, in this instance, a change in the semantic qualities of the phrase black dada nihilismus begins to become apparent. This phrase is an utterance of the inability to give a fair representation, as dada in poetry, and is also a returning to primitivism in language through the use of sounds rather than words as typically recognized. These utterances present the phenomenological dilemma or paradox described by Moten and represent—although I would argue incompletely—things unable to be represented by words. Furthermore, the working to overcome ambivalence is present by using words to represent things that cannot be represented by words by combining this idea of Dadaism with nihilism and blackness. If we return to Moten, it appears that the speaker is presenting the idea that black is itself pure negativity, thus it is necessary to reconstruct the meaning of black to change the way it is perceived.

The fifth stanza begins to move away from God and discusses stained glass as Mondrian (lines 10–11). It must be recognized that not only was Piet Mondrian a nonrepresentational artist, but also he was the founder of the De Stijl movement, otherwise known as the neoplasticism movement, where he "believed that abstraction was intellectually pure and 'natural.'"[26] This is significant because purity has often been reserved for Jesus Christ, as the mention of protestant love stated in line 10. By having the stained-glass window identified with Mondrian (line 11), it suggests that the only purity is through abstraction, which is akin to Dadaism in that it is a form of abstract art, but the purity moves from God to abstraction, each of which is also unrepresentable. Thus, the speaker is here flirting with the idea of the death of god and attempting to represent the unrepresentable, but this idea comes to full realization through the trauma inherent in the remainder of the stanza.

The second half of the fifth stanza discusses the death of Jews during surgery (lines 11–13). The proximity of this poem's publication to the Holocaust forces the reader to associate this line with that horrific event. By discussing the deaths of Jews, the speaker is utilizing traumatic figurative language to evoke associations among the Holocaust, the idea of the murder in the previous stanza, the death of god discussed earlier in this stanza, and the collapse of representation associated with black dada nihilismus. The stanza continues by presenting the next few lines inside an open parenthesis that has no closing mate. Although this may seem insignificant, this is symbolic of the very idea of representing trauma: we witness an event but are never granted closure. As opposed to the Jews who died under the surgeon's knife, that I would suggest refers indirectly to medical experiments of the Holocaust where industrialized genocide attempted to destroy the very culture and existence of the Jewish people, this waking on the street is separated by the parenthesis, thus the race and culture of the waking people is unknown. What is known is that they wake up with "money and a hip / nose" (lines 15–16), signifying that their nose was changed; given that we see blackness to be a nonrepresentation as Dada and nihilismus suggest, for the nose to be hip, it must be white. The plastic surgery to change the nose, which is symbolic for a changing of one's culture, whether the individuals are African American or Jewish, is rewarded rather than a billed surgical procedure. As such, the individuals are being rewarded for trying to lose their cultural identity.

In the sixth stanza, we encounter "Trilby," which may refer to a type of hat. However, more significantly, *Trilby* is a novel about a Jewish hypnotist who teaches the main character, Trilby, to sing. Trilby is unable to sing unless she is in a hypnotized state. Eventually, when the hypnotist dies, the spell is broken, and she remembers nothing of her singing career. Thus, Trilby has two identities: one she knows when in a normal state and one that exists when she is under hypnosis. This is significant in the poem, and in African American identity, because, before the Black Arts Movement, many blacks had an identity constructed around white American standards, yet it is their own identity that many are in search for. This is also key when we consider that the poem was written during Baraka's "Transitional Period" between his "Beat Period" and his "Black Nationalist Period," so the speaker, like many other African American writers of the 1960s, was attempting to construct a new identity but had yet to engage the Afro-centric, revolutionary aesthetic that would dominate the BAM. Thus, only by killing the oppressive superstructure of white control can African Americans "wake up" and understand their true identity. In this poem, however, the speaker moves the idea by insinuating the idea of African Americans are being used like Trilby in their films, hypnotized agents being exploited while the floors of the movie house become sticky (line 17) referring perhaps both to gluttonous actions where things are sloppily eaten or to the masturbatory practices that Baraka has spoken of in other poems. Either insinuation results in the same meaning: the (white) movie house presidents are benefiting and finding joy through the visual and imaginary exploitation of blacks. Later in the sixth stanza, the speaker mentions Hermes, which is a reference to not only the Greek god Hermes, who was the messenger between the gods and humans, but also to the art of hermeneutics, or the study of interpretation. To be black, then, is to be an interpreter within, and of, white culture—especially, as we have seen in the previous stanza, purity resides in abstractions, and black dada nihilismus urges people to defy the current modes of representation while attempting to articulate the unrepresentable. This articulation is not one meant to be therapeutic for a type of coping within the African American community, but one that refuses to conform or be readily understood by the eye of whiteness.

The speaker then turns his attention to the idea of thievery in line 19 and uses another opening parenthesis that has no closing mate. The unmated parenthesis refuses to allow closure of the ideas that are being presented. In this sense, much like trauma, closure is not something that comes by easily, if ever. The need to perpetuate the ideas inherent in the poem are reinforced by this, but the parenthesis also acts like open-ended quotation marks. In situations where the quotation continues into the next paragraph, closed quotations are not used until the end of the quoted passage. The use of open parenthesis here is similar, yet there is no closing, indicating that the voices of African Americans are not only not heard, but they are only understood parenthetically within the white cultural norm. The use of parenthesis also represents a kind of hiding of the text within the text, which exists because of white society's refusal to hear or listen to African Americans, and, especially, African American art.

The thieves and people searching for gold (line 20) referred to in this stanza are the Europeans that colonized North America in search of gold and riches. This is especially evident given the reference to Moctezuma in line 24. What is referenced here is historic trauma, as the lines referring to the thievery are mixed with the idea of Hermes and Trismegistus appearing in line 21. Hermes Trismegistus, it must be recognized, is a sacred being that is perceivable through divine revelation; thus, the speaker is playing off the idea of religion again yet begins discussing transmutations in line 22. This discussion of transmutations becomes most troubling as he refers to the bullets and past violence (line 23). As such, in the first portion of the poem, the speaker is referring to colonization and the looting and killing of people, which transformed the Americas, among other places (lines 24–25). The speaker is also using traumatic figurative language to compare the devastation of colonization, exploitation, and genocide perpetrated by the colonizers against the African people, which has ultimately destroyed the culture, leaving the ancestors groping to establish a culture of their own.

Black dada nihilismus is the result, as the speaker shows African Americans rejecting the current modes of representation and white standards in order to represent not only the black experience, but also cultural trauma, which encompasses a great deal of the black experience. This rejection of white standards is a resistance against those who attempt to judge African American art under this Eurocentric idea and those who attempt to describe blackness as a singular representation rather than multiplicity. Thus, the speaker, and indeed all those who wish to describe the historical black experience, has difficulty trying to discuss the experience through a new form of representation while attempting to represent the unrepresentable. This is key to not only this poem but to other poets of the Black Arts Movement. Poets such as Sonia Sanchez in books like *We A baddDDD People* and Haki R. Madhubuti's *Don't Cry, SCREAM* attempt to represent the black experience outside the white aesthetic experience by using nonstandard "white" English and by breaking up the traditional form of the poem by the use of the poem's placement on the page. Many poets also call on other African American-centered art forms in their poetry, especially jazz and the blues, in order to help articulate and celebrate the experience. Therefore, the white experience and white aesthetic standard are not the norm; in fact, they are to be worked against.

The second half of the poem begins by discussing Sartre, calling into doubt not his existentialism, but more precisely Sartre's belief in human freedom. This human freedom, as can easily be seen, has not included Africans or African Americans historically, nor during the time the poem was written, given the struggle of the Civil Rights Movement and the Black Arts Movement. The reason for the inclusion of Sartre in the poem resides in his belief in conjoining politics and art in order that art may help propel human improvement, just as the Black Arts Movement did. In addition, it should be noted that Sartre found himself physically under attack, which included his apartment building being the target of a bombing.[27] To return to the poem, the speaker suggests that using art to further a political cause is incredibly dangerous and to use art in this way, as the poem continues to discuss later, can lead to violence. At the same time, however, the speaker is begging Sartre to die. What is being engaged here is not just issues of freedom and responsibility, but the idea of Sartre's efforts to define ontology beyond the reach of culture and history. This is significant because it allows people like the speaker to imagine themselves outside the realms of white culture and the historical paradigm of whiteness, but at the same time, it denied the legitimacy of black culture and black history. It is black dada nihilismus, the attempt to represent and give a separate culture to an oppressed people, which lead to the death of Sartre, according to the poem. The plastique in line 29 is not only a play on Mondrian and neoplastique as mentioned earlier as well as the plastic surgery spoken of in lines 15 and 16, but also is referring to the attack on Sartre in 1961 as a plastique explosives bomb went off at his apartment building.[28] The speaker states he does not have such material, only razors (line 30).

The speaker asks in lines 32 through 40 why blacks do not rise up to overcome oppression. The speaker then turns his frustration stemming from historical trauma and distress associated with the need to express the black experience to violence against the white oppressor and blacks unwilling to advance the movement. The speaker personifies historical trauma in lines 39 through 42 by making the people who have suffered in the past rise from their graves and attack whites and blacks who do not advance the cause of establishing a black voice and black perspective. The raping and killing of whites (lines 41–42) and the killing of blacks who act subservient to whites (lines 45–46) are not only a call for an actual killing, but a killing of the white perspective that is the point of reference for the black experience. The fact that the lips are described as being the color of liver, presented on line 51, underscores the idea that incorporating the Eurocentric, white values that writers of the Black Arts Movement are working against is a type of poison that harms the authenticity of artistic expression in the black experience. By presenting this idea in this fashion, where the imagery alludes to fellatio, reinforces the negative aspect of incorporating white ideas and aesthetics to talk about the black experience. This homophobic imagery is problematic in its homophobia, but also refers to the demeaning nature that whites were treating blacks. Unless black artists and writers begin establishing their own artistic expression, African Americans will be seen as forever inferior, and forever the slave, as the white man mentioned here is referred to as master.

In the next stanza, the poem attempts to represent the unrepresentable by means of harnessing frustrations and emotions influenced by historical trauma. The speaker utilizes vocalizations, which are outside the scope of traditional white culture by producing new forms of utterance not recognized by white aesthetic. These screams, hollers, and chants are the utilization of expressions not only outside the traditional white recognition of art because of their legacy in African American culture but screaming and hollering are also forms of expression that exist as a reaction to pain and trauma (lines 47–54). In this manner, the screams and hollers represent both African American tradition as well as trauma. The poem continues by discussing how his people have learned callous ideas pressed upon them by the whites (lines 59–65). These ideas are the white ideals that the speaker is attempting to fight against and doing so for the African and African American musicians, artists, actors, and activists listed in lines 67 through 71.

The final stanza begins with the fourth and final opening parenthesis without a closing mate and prays to damballah, who is the voodoo god attributed with creating all life. Thus, a god who created the world, from a religion created by diasporic Africans, is prayed to, which is perfectly symbolic of the desire of the poem for creating something uniquely African American. The speaker asks to be saved from the murders that he hopes his followers will commit against white children (line 74) and ends with the repeated phrase, which is the title of the poem (line 75). The request to be saved and to be forgiven for their actions, by the god being spoken of, would likely be very understanding given that the god shares a common heritage and existence, being understood as neither African nor American. The use of voodoo here is another form of ambivalence in that voodoo is an amalgamation of aspects of African religious traditions and Christianity, yet it is both and neither. Furthermore, while this poem is repeatedly calling for death, the god called upon is one who creates life, for it is only through the death of the reliance on the white culture that African American culture and representation may gain life. Yet, so much of African American culture is intertwined with and is a result from a movement against white culture and a result of white trauma that the killing of the white cultural norm is something both to strive against yet difficult to overcome. Because of these aspects, African American culture is always already tied to white culture. The ambivalence in how to proceed is not inherent within the speaker, but within the poem itself. Like the protestant love spoken in line 10 just before the deaths of Jews spoke in line 12, the protestant religion builds off of the Jewish faith, just as African American culture is tied to white culture. As such, the speaker is again calling for a moving away from the point of reference of white America and instead asking for a new form of representation; through the destruction of white culture, the experience of a black cultural experience can emerge. The chantlike, repetitive quality of the phrase "black dada nihilismus," as it exists in the poem, is significant in how it represents the struggle to articulate the black experience. By being presented in a manner similar to a chant, it harkens to an earlier culture while also working against what is considered art and is thus working against the oppressive white culture. Importantly, the nonrepresentational representation of what is unrepresentable continually reemerges, mimicking the brain's repeating of traumatic events in order to attempt comprehension. "Black Dada Nihilismus" is not only an idea and a poem, but also a representation of trauma and a burgeoning form of expression of African America attempting to produce and reproduce a black voice, both artistic and political.

Many of Baraka's poems represent trauma, often in the form of imagery, such as the lynching imagery in his poem "Reggae or Not,"[29] which includes such lines as "our women watched when the crackers cut off our balls / in the grass, they made the little girls watch / stuffed them in our mouths" (lines 38–40). In other poems, images of slavery are readily apparent. In addition, several of Baraka's poems use nonsensical words in the form of screams to express that which is impossible to convey in purely semantic terms. In "Reggae or Not," screams occur in lines near episodes of trauma such as terror (lines 66–67), which is the continuation of the lynching description. In both instances, the speaker's inability to articulate the feelings associated with those traumas is transformed into a scream, representing what cannot be represented by words alone. What is occurring here, if we refer to Moten, is very similar to Moten's discussion of refusing to reproduce the account of Aunt Hestor's beating in Fredrick Douglass's narrative, is the presentation of emotion and reaction through a scream rather than the telling of emotion. In his introduction, he is examining Saidiya V. Hartman's *Scenes of Subjection: Terror, Slavery, and Self-Making in Nineteenth-Century America*[30] and her discussion of Frederick Douglass's slave narrative. In Moten's text, he discusses how although Hartman does not reproduce the account of the violent event, "it is reproduced in her referent to and refusal of it; second, the beating is reproduced in every scene of subjection the book goes on to read."[31] Moten makes clear that he is not suggesting that Hartman tried and could not make the violent account disappear. Instead he states, "Hartman's considerable, formidable, and rare brilliance is present in the space she leaves for the ongoing (re)production of that performance in all its guises and for a critical awareness of how each of those guises is always already present in and disruptive of the supposed originality of that primal scene."[32] Baraka's poem is producing something similar by presenting screams in "Reggae or Not." Rather than discuss the anguish, frustration, and distress associated with such violent events, the speaker in Baraka's poem allows these emotions to exist in a vacuum created by this scream. In the place of discussing the pain, torment, and frustration, the speaker fills this void with a scream. Like Hartman, Baraka's poem creates and reproduces massive stressors and distress by not directly discussing the emotions. This is significant because it is insinuating that the articulation of the distress felt by the speaker and the discussion of these particular massive stressors cannot aptly be represented, thus the speaker has resorted to articulations that reside outside the bounds of semantic registers.

This is also an articulation that resides outside the cultural understanding and aesthetic and intellectual registers of white America. This is an utterance by a black speaker, for a black audience, about historical black trauma and current black frustrations. This is a break in the poem, away from words, existing in the poetic equivalent of scat in jazz, where there is both a breakdown, and more importantly for the Black Arts Movement, a movement beyond words for representation into a new mode of understanding. Both of these articulations by the speakers are attempting to articulate the massive stressors and distress, yet the means in which this can aptly be presented escapes the speaker. This harkens back to Moten, as he states, "There is no phenomenology, only phenomenological problems—and to notice in passing that noticing an aspect—a phenomenological problem that, as we shall see, demands *description* in light of its exceeding of *explanation*—is in the aftermath or wake of this formation: not but of not but of not but of."[33] The speaker is attempting to describe an event and the feeling of distress, yet this articulation is in a perpetual state of deferment, and the speaker in this poem can only partially describe what has occurred yet understands that a sufficient description of the events and massive stressors associated with the event transcend representation. This is *not* an attempt on behalf of the poet to transfer the feeling of anxiety to the reader but is the presentation of feelings and frustrations manifested in a scream where the *speaker* is unable to formulate the words to express the trauma that has manifested inside. This technique is not the expression of the speaker's own personal trauma, but the quasi-verbalization of historical trauma, which continues to affect the speaker. In the performance of the poem, such an expression of emotion and breakdown in semantic registers will greatly affect his audience, more so, I believe, than his readership. The expression of trauma is significant because Baraka's speaker is demonstrating, through the screams, how the historical trauma has affected the speaker, yet this technique does not directly tell the audience that he or she has suffered trauma but refers to suffering in a collective *we* as demonstrated in lines 135–136.

This technique has the potential to show the reader and listeners how trauma of the past can influence people of the present and may call on the reader to act. The audience may be encouraged to fight against the oppression and racism they encounter daily and move the Black Power political movement forward. Furthermore, the artists and writers in the audience, who understanding the importance of attempting to bring forth a representation of the black experience of the Black Arts Movement, may witness the movement away from traditional representational strategies, as Baraka's speakers do by abandoning all semantic forms of language, and strive to further the establishment of the black experience in America, while also calling upon centuries of historical trauma.

Another of Baraka's poems that effectively demonstrates abjection and unhomeliness is "Legacy," published in his 1969 book *Black Magic*. Baraka's *Black Magic* was the first book published after what William J. Harris calls his "Black Nationalist Period"[34] and expressed sentiments of black nationalism, which Baraka embraced four years previous to the book's publication. Baraka's poem "Legacy" presents the imagery of African Americans struggling to live in the American South, and it attempts to find ways to escape the massive stressors and torment of their situation. It is apparent from the outset, with the title of the poem "Legacy," and the first line of the poem, that the poem is focusing on the legacy of Southern slavery, which directly lead to the racism still present in the United States today. The second hint that this is a glimpse into the lives of a group of African Americans appears in lines 13 and 14 where the speaker discusses traveling to different towns that are inhabited by African Americans. These lines are recalling the travel of people from one town to another. The poem begins by situating the location of the poem in the South, yet the word "south" is not capitalized. This creates a bit of confusion in that the American South is identified with the first letter being capitalized, as it is a proper place. By not capitalizing this letter, the speaker is not limiting the location of the poem to the American South, insinuating that such a situation could occur anywhere, yet given the epigraph dedicates the poem to blues people, which is properly capitalized, the idea that the location is wherever African Americans would reside, the American South or the southern parts of cities. The people of the poem are shown sleeping in various locations (lines 1–3) and others are shown "stumbling" (line 3). They are doing so while being observed (lines 4–5) as if always under the watchful eye of whites and law enforcement.

In the next line they are "drunk waving moving a hand or lash" (line 6). Both sleeping and drinking are behaviors which allow an individual to escape from the stress associated with daily life, and this is especially significant given that they are said to be sleeping against a drugstore, where many people go for help for an ailment. It is evident that those mentioned have no access to these aids. Although the mention of these activities is used to present the image of escape and coping against massive stressors associated with historical trauma, the most common motif used within the poem is abjection and unhomeliness.

When examining the images, it is important to note that in none of the activities are people shown at their homes. This is significant because many of the activities, such as the person sleeping in the first line, would be expected to occur at home. There is a lack of a home presented within the poem, and with the amount of movement, especially in the final portion of the poem, it becomes apparent that abjection is a strong factor present within the poem, not only for the riders of the horses but also for others within the poem. The first instance of movement occurs with the stumbling that occurs at the end of line 3. However, the stumbling is never attributed to one or more people; therefore, it is impossible to ascertain the number of people stumbling in this manner. Given that the people are mentioned sleeping and in a drunken state, the stumbling is associated with these people moving through life in a stupor related to their chosen mental escape.

This is different than the type of abjection found in the previous chapter on Japanese Americans who were forced from their home and placed in encampments. The individuals in this poem, because they are African American, had no home from the beginning. By being African American, they are always already unhomed and existing in a dispossessed state of existence without a physical home, and equally important for the Black Arts Movement, no home culture or representation was part of their experience, except mythically and memorially (e.g., Africa). Slaves were never guaranteed safety, security, or stability in their quarters, nor were they recognized as familial units, many of whom were separated through sales. Even after slavery, racist laws, landlords, and communities, as well as the need for work, often lead to transient existences for many. In addition, during the time of this poem's creation, the establishment of a cultural home was on the forefront of the minds of people; thus, the home being sought is as much cultural as physical and emotional.

The traumatic imagery of the poem begins to unfold after the mention of stumbling with the image of person "drunk waving moving a hand or lash" (line 6). It is uncertain whether the drunken figure spoken of in line 6 is one of those stumbling or not; regardless, this person is reacting to a past trauma, indicated by the word lash, which ends line 6. The inclusion of lash (line 6) recalls historic traumas associated with whips and beatings. However, the frowning person is the one wielding the hand or lash, so it is he or she who is perpetrating the violence, which could be an allusion to slaves who were made foremen and who had the job of beating slaves in order to discipline them. The traumatic language continues in the next line as we see the transformation in the activities described: "Dancing kneeling reaching out, letting / a hand rest in shadows" (lines 7–8). Although the line starts with "Dancing" (line 7), the action immediately changes to "kneeling" (line 7) and "reaching out" (line 7), which is indicative of a type of submission, either to a deity or someone in a position of authority. If we consider the lash from the previous line and how the wielder of the lash could have been an allusion to a foreman who beat slaves, the people kneeling and reaching out could be doing so to ask for forgiveness from either a deity or person/people because of his actions. The fact that he is "letting / a hand rest in shadows" (lines 7–8) demonstrates that his hand is still residing in the collective, cross-cultural guilt of wrongdoing in the past, and potentially in the present, since part of him is reaching out for forgiveness while his hand resides in the darkness of negativity, illustrated by the shadows. The hand in the shadows is a metaphor for the historic trauma still plaguing the culture today.

As the poem continues, the next images are of an individual also close to the ground as they squat (lines 8–9). With the overlapping and uninterrupted flow of images, the poem becomes both confusing and partially fragmented as the images of people are presented and suddenly change. The image of the dancing, kneeling, reaching person just examined quickly changes to an individual squatting. As with the other images within the poem, it is not clear whether or not the individuals who are squatting are the same as those kneeling. The next image is of individuals, as we are given indication of more than one for the first time since line 3, who are getting on horses to ride to the sea (line 11). Following this image, the speaker then presents the second half of this line and first part of the next in parentheses, which makes the event appear suspect by calling it a song (lines 11–12). By presenting the idea in this manner, it makes it appear as myth or legend, quite similar to the poem by Inada. The sea does not appear again until the final line, and it becomes known that the myth is not about the people, but the sea (line 17) that the riders are trying to find. Given the significance of the Middle Passage, slave ships, and the oceanic slave trade, the sea is a very loaded image. As the speaker refers to "the old song" here, with the poem's title ("Legacy") and epigraph ("*For Blues People*"), the speaker is referring to slave spirituals, work songs, the blues, jazz, and traditional African songs that may still exist within community or minds of the individuals. The sea, when sung in the spirituals, often referred to Moses and the Israelites. The American slaves were well aware of the diasporic Israelites and saw parallels in their plight. Calling upon the sea in these songs would not only have been a reference to the slave ships and crossing of the Atlantic, but a reference to the miracle performed by Moses for the Israelites. This resounded as hope within the song of the enslaved of freedom, either in life or in death. The speaker, by referring to it as pretend and suspect, is discounting this hope. The ultimate goal is to reach the sea, which is symbolic for finding peace and identity, but the sea is pretend, thus peace and identity are unattainable. The poem is discussing a flawed hope in something (freedom) that does not, cannot, and never has existed.

Even in the face of this despondency, there are still those who attempt to find the sea that the speaker does not believe in. In the poem, as the riders mount the horses, they are traveling to different African American towns (lines 13–14). The repetition of moving from one town to another town, similar to the one they just left, creates a feeling that the change the riders seek is unattainable. This is compounded by the mention of the sea being pretend in line 17 and by the way the sea is mythologized in lines 11 and 12. As the poem continues, the riders find more people sleeping (line 14). This town, much like the one they left, is similar, not only in its cultural makeup, but in the actions of the inhabitants. The inhabitants of the new town, which the riders are passing through, are encountering the world in the "disoriented and fragmented" state of abjection as identified by Fuchs.[35] The riders, who are searching for the sea, are presented in a state of unhomeliness, in some other place than the sea that they are attempting to find, and, as well, every person in the poem is presented in an unhomely state of abjection. This idea is perpetuated in line 16 where, rather than the speaker mentioning houses, which might give a sense of homeliness to the poem, the poem presents an image of the houses' shadows. In this manner, the poem is presenting the intangible presence of houses, but they exist outside the grasp of the people within the poem. The image of the shadow is significant especially when one considers its representation of historical trauma in line 8. Therefore, not only are the individuals in the poem without homes, but the homes of others reinforce historical trauma within the wandering culture. The sea that the wanderers are in search of represents not only hope, but home. The sea is what separated the slaves from their homeland, and by searching for the sea, the wanderers may be able to find not only the sea that divides them from their ancestral home, but, to continue with the sea being a metaphor for hope, the hope for a new home.

The ambivalence presented in the second to last line, along with the word "pretended," that is describing the sea, mars the hope presented in the last line. The people are moving toward one of two very distinct things within this line: the moon or shadows that were created by houses that exist outside of town, where people sleep. These two images represent distinctly different situations for those leaving the town. By moving toward the moon, they are following a path of light, although lesser than that provided by the sun, in order to find a home. This moving by moonlight is reminiscent of the flight taken by those of the Underground Railroad, thus this path not only gives homage to their ancestors but represents a Great Migrationesque travel, which will lead the people away from the town and, perhaps, the region. The other option presented is to live in the shadows of the people living in the town. Living in the shadow has its own cliché connotation; however, the idea of shadows also signifies mimicry. As such, the line presents a decision to those leaving or staying, but the poem fails to give reason to do either, thus the ambivalence signifies that it doesn't matter which is selected, for the sea is nonexistent by being "pretended" (line 17).

This same ambivalence exists earlier in the poem where people are said to be squatting, but they are identified as either drinking or urinating (lines 8-9). By not distinguishing this, like the destination discussed earlier, it is as if it doesn't matter. Furthermore, it suggests that the people could be ingesting the waste of others. This occurs just after the mention of the hand in the shadow, which reinforces the idea of historical trauma, and before the mention of sea in line 11. These instances of ambivalence demonstrate not only a sense of hopelessness but dejection. The sea, a major motif in African American literature related to the Middle Passage, has been removed from reality, with different liquids mentioned indicating new problems, not unrelated to the old traumas of the past, yet neither of which has a resolve. The present is still impacted by the past, but one of the main problems resides in how the people are called to move toward a sea that doesn't exist because they are still listening to the same song (lines 10, 16). The answer in how to overcome the legacy is both given and not given.

The speakers in Baraka's poetry, like the speakers of other poets examined thus far, utilize motifs specific to literary trauma theory, such as abjection and unhomeliness, to engage traumas and massive stressors associated with racism. Although the two Baraka poems examined are not necessarily representative of all the works of Baraka (such an endeavor is far beyond the scope of this study), these two poems are highly representative of the focus on trauma as well as the need to express the black experience in the United States. Taken from early in the Black Arts Movement, these poems attempt to represent that which could not be aptly represented in regard to a culture striving to use a means of expression beyond the oppressive white society as well as trauma, both of which are fundamentally tied to one another. Other poems by Baraka, as well as other poems coming from the African American community, engage these issues because the idea of expressing what it means to be black in the United States is a crucial issue but is always already tied to historical trauma, regardless if the poet wants to engage the issue. Some poets and poems do not, but for those that do, the use of traumatic figurative language, abjection, unhomeliness, and other poetic motifs of literary trauma theory are beneficial to expressing these emotions but are often found in the poetry regardless if they were used consciously.

ABJECTION, FRAGMENTATION, ISOLATION, AND UNHOMELINESS IN THE POETRY OF LUCILLE CLIFTON

As discussed, Baraka's poems engages with the historical trauma inherent within African America, and as he produces writings that speak of the black experience in the United States, he must engage the historical trauma because of its intrinsic place in the black experience, both negatively and in terms of empowering the black nation. Elements of trauma can be found in several of Lucille Clifton's poems from the collection *Good Times* published in 1969. In the poetry from this collection, Clifton's speakers not only engage trauma and the black experience, but isolation. This is a common characteristic, both reactionary and self-imposed, by survivors of trauma because of the overwhelming feeling that no one can understand the feelings she is going through because of what they have witnessed. The distress endured by attempting to reconcile historical traumas associated with one's ancestors, and trauma that may still be apparent when the poem was composed, have the potential to reinforce this feeling of isolation. The poetry of Clifton presents this isolation, and it is a frequent motif found within her poetry, hence the selection of her for this study. Clifton's poems "the inner city," "my mama moved among the days," and "if something should happen" each present isolation as well as other poetic devices common in literary trauma theory. Furthermore, when one considers the need to express the black experience in the Black Arts Movement, it is apparent that isolation plays an important role. The artists wishing to discuss the black experience must isolate themselves from the white aesthetic but are also already isolated from white society because they are black. Thus, it is important to engage isolation, not only when engaging trauma, but the black experience.

Since her death in 2010, several articles have been written about Lucille Clifton focusing on feminism, such as Rachel Elizabeth Harding's "Authority, History, and Everyday Mysticism in the Poetry of Lucille Clifton: A Womanist View," [36] Scarlett Cunningham's "The Limits of Celebration in Lucille Clifton's Poetry: Writing the Aging Woman's Body,"[37] and Emilia Tetty Harjani's "The Feminist Voice in Lucille Clifton's 'The Thirty Eighth Year,' 'Miss Rosie' and 'Final Note to Clark.'"[38] Other critics examined her poetry by discussing religion in her poetry "The Light That Came to Lucille Clifton: Beyond Lucille and Lucifer,"[39] while others wrote articles celebrating her life, like Toi Derricotte's "Won't You Celebrate with Me: Remembering Lucille Clifton."[40] However, very little has been written about the trauma inherent within Clifton's poetry.

The feelings of unhomeliness and ambivalence are also present in the first poem of Clifton's book *Good Times*. The poem is untitled but begins with the line "in the inner city."[41] The poem refers, as the first line indicates, to the inner city (lines 2–4). At this point, it is evident that the speaker and those whom she is referring to have a home, the inner city, but as the poem progresses, this residence is not actually one that the speaker considers home. As the poem continues, the speaker shows that they still think of other places, which as can be seen in line 6, that are more peaceful. This image of "uptown" (lines 5) is next described by having "houses straight as / dead men" (lines 7–8). By the houses appearing straight (line 7), the order that is inferred from the silence from uptown is continued in line 6. This idea quickly takes a different connotation as line 7 compares the straightness of the homes to "dead men" (line 8). The negativity associated with death and the houses being as "straight as / dead men" (lines 7–8) makes problematic the idea of uptown (line 5) being a hopeful candidate for home, so the speaker is ambivalent in what she and those around her want. The speaker states that she and others think about the life that could be had uptown but understands the danger. The peace that is said to be uptown is found in the word "silent" (line 6) and could represent a place of less stress, strife, and danger, but the very peace could also suggest their own death, as represented dead men in line 8. As such, the ambiguity of uptown leads to ambivalence for the reader as she thinks about that very place.

The most telling line associated with ambivalence and unhomeliness occurs in line 10 as the speaker feels that their home is no place. Even though they have a place to reside, neither this place nor the calm uptown are places they consider home. In the next line, the speaker proclaims that she and the others are "happy to be alive" (line 11). Although this happiness is not indicative of happiness in the peoples' lives, it is happiness "to be *alive*" (line 11, my emphasis). Given the comparison of the houses to dead men in lines 7 and 8, this line provides great contrast to the silence of uptown and suggests that the speaker and others are happy just to be alive. The happiness here is not an emotion of joy, but a feeling of being thankful for still having one's life. Presenting the uptown houses and neighborhood, as well as residents, as dead is commentary on white culture, which is in contrast to the vivacity, thus succinct celebration, of the black, yet unhomely, culture celebrated by the happiness to be alive the speaker presents. The final four lines are a repetition of the first four lines, which include the previous line about the inner city (lines 13–15). As stated, this happiness is not joy, but the feeling of being thankful, thus the speaker and others are thankful to have a place to reside, the inner city, yet this is not, nor will be, a place that can be considered home. This thankfulness is not shared in the white communities because they do not understand happiness that goes along with being thankful just to be alive. In addition, the speaker is thankful to be alive in the celebration of African American culture as opposed to the silent, dead culture the speaker perceives as existing in the white neighborhoods.

The repetition of the first four lines, as they close the poem, is significant because they are repetitive, and because they occur at the opening and closing of the poem, this suggests that life in the inner city is cyclical. The overall structure of the poem, with its short lines and small stature, forces the reader to pay very close attention to each word. Although this is often expected of poetry, in this case, the longest line is only eight words, and the phrases within the lines jump out to the reader with the centermost line being most striking. Line 8, composed of only two words, "dead men," is surrounded by the longest lines of the poem. The placement of this line in the inner most portion of the poem is not coincidental, especially given the speaker's repetition and emphasis on the inner city. By placing "dead men" (line 8) in the center of the poem, this is analogous to the people she speaks of being in the inner city. In this way, the speaker is suggesting that lives of those in the inner city are perilous, and the fact they are thankful to be alive is a more logical supposition on the poetic persona's behalf.

The structure of the poem, with short lines and several lines consisting of only one or two lines, forces the reader quickly down the page. This suggests that the life is fast for those living in the inner city, either in the fact that death could come early or indicating the quickness of what is going around in the area. The absolute center of the poem (line 8 of 16) is the line reading "dead men." Not only is the reader's eye immediately drawn to this line and phrase, but it signifies that death is a central component of life in the inner city. It is a dangerous place for those who live there and for anyone who enters. The only other lines that are composed of just one word contain the words "or" and "home." Therefore, the choice that one has is either to call the inner-city home or become dead men. Thus, even though the inner city may not feel like home, that is where the speaker must reside.

The idea of unhomeliness continues in the next poem of the collection, although the sentiments of abjection, while often existent alongside unhomeliness, are most predominant in Clifton's poem beginning, "my mama moved among the days."[42] Similar to other poems by Clifton, this poem lacks a title and will be referenced by the first line. The movement in the poem, as apparent in the first line, begins immediately. The second line transforms the movement into abjection as we see that the mother is moving "like a dreamwalker" (line 2). To be a dreamwalker (line 2) is similar to Fuchs's definition of a "blinded, maze-walker";[43] therefore, mama (line 1) in Clifton's poem, moves through the field in a manner that has no true destination, as can be seen later in the poem, and she is also influenced by dreams, which relates strongly to trauma. The subject of the poem is significant in that she is the mother of the speaker: she represents the historical heritage of the speaker, and as demonstrated in lines 3 and 4, she takes on superior, perhaps even mythological, qualities.

Mama is described in the next two lines as having abilities that allow her to be impervious to the world around her and also as having a great influence over everything she encounters (lines 3–4). The mythology created around mama is significant, not only because she is representative of cultural heritage, but because of her inability to be harmed by that by which she is touched. Mama is able to navigate the "high grass" (line 5) even though she is moving through the field like a "dreamwalker" (line 2). The field navigation and high grass are part of the metaphor used to describe mama's movement through days, thus time. The navigation of daily activities is difficult, and although mama navigated in the manner of abjection, she is able to help those with her. As has been stated, mama is representative of historical culture, so the speaker is only able to navigate the stresses and difficulties in life by the aid of historical culture. Moreover, the character of mama is doubly significant in the empowerment not only of African Americans but of African American women. The Black Arts Movement was not especially progressive in its attitude toward women, thus the speaker is provoking two powerful implications through her character of mama. First, mama's inability to leave the high grass is commentary on the Black Power movement leaving women behind in the quest for equality and empowerment. This is highly significant because she is suggesting a double oppression that is readily understood in the context of minority women. Secondly, the speaker is empowering African American women by having mama be the facilitator to aid others as they attempt to navigate the massive historical stressors that affect African Americans. Mama is the strong leader, and the speaker is suggesting that the women of African American culture are the ones who can heal and lead the culture past the influence of the historically traumatic stressors. This trauma is also apparent in the use of repetition.

The poem repeats several words and phrases throughout the poem and places these repetitions close together so as to easily draw the reader's attention to the repetition. Furthermore, the repeated use of the word "like" and "seemed like" creates ambivalence in the poem, in addition to presenting actual repetition. Rather than having the qualities, the character of mama is described as if she "seemed like" she had them. The lack of assurance creates this ambivalence, which sets up the last portion of the poem as the character of mama takes a peculiar turn in the final portion of the poem. In line 6, the speaker sees mama change her direction just before the speaker finds the edge of the field. In line 5, the word "almost" is essential to the meaning of the line, indicating that they did not make it through. The aid of mama is only able to get the speaker so far, and as seen in the next line, mama turns back (lines 6–8). Mama seems unsure whether to leave the field or return. She is ambivalent in how to proceed and is said to reenter the grass. It is within the final three lines that the poem focuses on repetition, figuratively, as the character mama returns to the difficulties of the high grass and show the actual repetition existent in the seventh and eighth lines. This repetition is highly suggestive of trauma and also shows the character of mama returning to the massive stressors represented by the tall grass, thus making the abjection indicated earlier more significant. Rather than understanding mama to be representative of just cultural heritage, as she returns to the massive stressors of the high grass, mama is also representative of cultural trauma. The abject state of the character of mama, and her repetitive nature, present her as an archetypal example of traumatic characteristics, and the fact that she resides and refuses to leave the massive stressors representative of the high grass reinforce this representation and ambivalence. Mama is also, as has been stated, an important figure in African American women empowerment. She is not only leading people through the traumatic stressors, but she chooses to return to help others, much like Harriet Tubman. This underscores the resilience of African American women, not only in their resolve to persevere through difficult circumstances, but to be selfless in their choices.

It must also be recognized that mama is isolating herself as she refuses to leave the high grass. She exists in a fragmented isolation, which is only broken up as she attempts to aid those individuals who are lost and trying to find their way. Mama is a martyr attempting to save others so that they do not face the same painful isolation that she faces. Enduring historical trauma can make one feel as though they are isolated, especially by the oppressive culture that remains in power. Mama also becomes symbolic for the art and expressions of the Black Arts Movement as such because it is this art and its political ties that can move African Americans out of the confusion of the tall grass to the realization of self and African American culture. Mama must be isolated because the black experience can only be understood in an aesthetic manner if removed from the white aesthetic. Such removal and presentation of the black experience also provides wisdom. Mama also moves beyond the traditional Black Arts Movement and empowers women, especially African American women because, as we can see by her representation in the poem, it is through the strength of African American women, the poem suggests, that the culture will endure the difficulties that surround them.

The speaker uses historical trauma and cultural heritage in order to navigate present stresses, and through such wisdom, we are shown that one can endure the stresses of daily life. The hope inspired by the mythical characteristics of mama, as exhibited in lines 3 and 4, allows the speaker and others to transcend the stresses that may infringe upon their abilities to negotiate their daily activities. As such, historical trauma is not only something that must be endured, but as the speaker demonstrates in this poem, the events of the past also may aid individuals as they engage stressors of the present, inspired by hope. In Clifton's final poem to be examined, "if something should happen," the message is not just for African Americans, but for whites, as the speaker

Chapter Three 97

gives a very ominous warning not to fight the change occurring in the Black Arts Movement or the empowerment of African Americans. In great contrast to mama in the previous poem, the people in "if something should happen" are not interested in healing but in the destruction of opposition. This destruction is much more in line with the ideas of destroying the white aesthetic in the Black Arts Movement and one that needs to be engaged before concluding the chapter. In this poem, there is a call for uprising in hopes of creating political and historical trauma to all, especially whites.

The traces of historical trauma inherent within Clifton's poem "if something should happen"[44] appear in the form of images and traumatic figurative language. The poem is one continuous stanza that can be broken into three sections that show different scenes. The first scene shows a boat on the ocean (lines 2–3). In these lines, the sea is tumultuous, and this recurs as a constant image throughout the poem. In the next two lines, the speaker continues the question associated with the title and first few lines, asking what would happen if the sea crashes (lines 4–5). Although it is evident that the crashing sea breaks the cargo, the idea of the cargo breaking against the sea (line 5) rather than the sides of the boat is somewhat confusing. As the poem continues, lines two through five are nearly repeated with the word chains replacing sea in line 7. By having the chains break and fall to the decks (line 8) rather than the ocean, this is suggestive that the cargo is human cargo, or slaves, which brings forth traumatic history. This idea of the cargo being human is validated later in the poem, so to consider the cargo here as slaves is not conjecture. Like the previous lines, there is similar repetition through these lines with the replacement of only a few words so that, instead of the cargo breaking against the side of the sea (lines 4–5), in lines 9 and 10 the sea is broken against the sides of the boat. These lines also suggest the sea as a representation of natural order attempting to break the unnatural, tyrannical dominance of man over man. The difference here, although subtle, presents the sea breaking rather than the cargo as in lines 4 and 5. The recombination of these words in these lines is significant poetically because the interaction of these words, and what they represent, create an effect whereas the trauma of the slave trade on the African captives as well as the slave traders, as agents, all become interconnected as a human trauma. The actions of the slave trade, and slavery, itself, resulted in highly engrained racism that has yet to untangle to this day. The sea, as will be demonstrated later on, is the sea of humanity; thus, the poem, and poets, for that matter, move beyond the scope of a singular race or group and speak to a more universal theme against hate and racism.

The crux of the poem resides in the final scene where the seas spoken of in line 12 are not saltwater but people. The poem presents a sea of people crashing against one another and suggests that if that were to occur, it would "break the chains" (line 14). This scenario varies greatly from the previous two scenes. In this instance, the people who have been oppressed, indicated by the chains breaking, become free through a sort of clash of peoples, suggestive of upheaval or revolution leading to a universal freedom for all humankind. In this scene, the people "break the chains / and break the walls holding down the cargo / and break the sides of the seas" (lines 14–16), which indicates the idea of the people rising up and taking material goods in a type of riot, symbolically rebelling against hegemonic power structures of the oppressors. The poem continues following the action of the sea and the people as the speaker suggests that this should be a worldwide occurrence where all oppressed people rise and revolt (lines 17–18). Line 16 is clearly connected to the lines previous, which speak of breaking the chains but are less a call to riot and action than a call for overcoming the differences of the various races and cultures of humankind. The sea becomes a type of equalizer, a force greater than any, where all must learn to swim or all drown together. Lines 17 and 18 continue in this call for equality where all the people of the world are said to come together (line 18). Upon closer examination, this breaking, which is repeated throughout the poem, is not the destructive action, but a symbolic destruction of ideologies that oppress different peoples as well as a call to establish a new aesthetic that is focused on the black experience. This idea becomes most apparent in the last two lines when the speaker asks where the leader will run (lines 19–20). These lines further implicate the sea to be not the literal oceanic water but rather the masses of oppressed people, the sea of humanity. The sea of people causes the captains, who represent the power elite, to run; thus those in power, by having to run, become the unhomed and diasporic. The white aesthetic must be destroyed and overthrown if there is to be a black culture and a black aesthetic.

When read in this manner, the first portion of the poem becomes less confusing, and the scene looks a great deal like the Boston Tea Party as the people crash upon the deck of a ship, go below decks, and break the cargo against the sea (line 4–5). The idea of the cargo breaking against the side of the sea then becomes a more tangible image of the captive and the oppressed having their lot thrown in with the greater corpus of humanity and attain a sort of freedom through equalization with the masses. However, one must remember that that sea is a mass of people, and thus a closer reading reveals that this could be both the literal and metaphorical ocean as the previous event discussed and a sort of looting of goods in the form of imperialism and a rebellion against imperialism in the form of the dissolution of the slave trade. If one accepts this latter understanding of the poem, then what is being presented is the formation of this country and the exploitation and genocide of the Native Americans. Thus, the reader is witnessing a comparison between the Native American genocide and African American enslavement in a form of figurative traumatic language. This interpretation is only partially correct when the poem is read in its entirety. The repetition of breaking the sides of the sea is of great significance, and it is clear that this action represents the breaking of the symbolic walls that keep a people oppressed. Thus, the first portion of the poem is also discussing the breaking of material inequality, which read alongside the idea of imperialism, is the inequality as a product of exploitation. This exploitation is also an exploitation of African Americans in the arts, thus a call to stop self-exploitation for the benefit of whites and to keep black art black.

The idea of imperialism becomes more evident in the second scene as it clearly discusses slavery. The second scene discusses the breaking of chains upon a ship, which is a description, not only of a slave ship, but the mutiny aboard a slave ship, much like what occurred on the *Amistad*. The chains, as are clearly represented within the text, are broken and the sea (9–10) is again broken. By rising up against those who keep the people oppressed, the oppressed can gain equality. The boat in this poem subverts the power of those on the slave ship as a way to sail to a symbolic freedom. Both scenes, in this poem, are calling on concealed presentations of historical trauma, with each taking a form of traumatic figurative language. The third scene is calling for an uprising of people in order to gain equality and is using these types of historical events as examples. Moreover, it is presenting these types of historical traumas to discuss the situation in which oppressed people find themselves. This freedom is also the idea of breaking away from the white aesthetic while creating art to represent the black experience. The speaker is calling on African Americans to continue forward in the Black Arts Movement and, perhaps more importantly, calling them to rise up politically.

As discussed, Clifton's poetry presents examples of abjection, isolation, and unhomeliness while narrating historical trauma. Feelings of unhomeliness and isolation are evident in her poem beginning "my mama moved among the days." Within both poems, the unhomeliness is portrayed and suggests unresolved historical trauma inherent within individuals within the poem. Although "my mama moved among the days" does utilize a metaphor in discussing the historical trauma, this metaphor is not a type of traumatic figurative language because the metaphor is not comparing the event with a traumatic event that occurred in the past in order to articulate the trauma that is taking place. In Clifton's poem "if something should happen," the speaker does utilize traumatic figurative language, but the poem does so in a concealed manner where, superficially, the comparison is with the ocean and a ship; however, upon deeper analysis, it becomes evident that the speaker is referring back to slavery and the Native American genocide. Each of Clifton's poems examines traumas, either historical or direct, felt by people, not only from African America, as presented here, but from other cultures. Each of Clifton's poems in this section utilizes isolation, a motif that is more prevalent in the poetry of Clifton than many other poets. This isolation not only demonstrates the remnants of historical trauma still inherent within African American culture but calls for a self-imposed isolation that would help in the advancement in an African American culture that existed outside the white aesthetic. The need to write and create art that was truly African American and escaped the Western cultural aesthetic was intrinsic to the ideas of the Black Arts Movement. The speakers of Clifton's poems were able to produce such a message and do so in a manner both positive and calming, as in "my mama moved among the days" as well as in a call for uprising in "if something should happen."

The poems of the Black Arts Movement that have been examined in this study exceed the bounds of literary trauma theory by advancing the idea of revolutionary empowerment through the exploration and poetic re-creation of trauma. The poetry in the following chapter is very similar in this regard. Each of these cultures is calling upon historical trauma and massive stressors that continue to afflict the people of both African American and Native American cultures. Recalling historical traumas allows the poets to encourage the establishment of an artistic voice outside of the oppressive white culture and call for political empowerment. In the next chapter, it is evident that poets are mediators in the Native American culture, just as they have been for the Japanese Americans and African Americans. The poets in the following section, some of whom were influenced by the American Indian Movement, allow for insight into trauma and distress by discussing a universal understanding of stressors. Furthermore, just as with the poets of the Black Arts Movement, the poets in the following chapter are calling for empowerment of Native Americans as they discuss traumas of the past.

NOTES

1. Ron Eyerman, *Cultural Trauma: Slavery and the Formation of African American Identity* (Cambridge: Cambridge University Press, 2001), 2.
2. Eyerman, *Cultural Trauma*, 1–2.
3. Larry Neal, "The Black Arts Movement," in *Within the Circle: An Anthology of African American Literary Criticism from the Harlem Renaissance to the Present*, ed. Angelyn Mitchell (Durham: Duke University Press, 1994), 184.

4. Hoyt W. Fuller, "Towards a Black Aesthetic," in *Within the Circle: An Anthology of African American Literary Criticism from the Harlem Renaissance to the Present*, ed. Angelyn Michell (Durham, NC: Duke University Press, 1994), 204.

5. Fuller, "Towards a Black Aesthetic," 204.

6. LeRoi Jones, "The Myth of a 'Negro Literature,'" in *Within the Circle: An Anthology of African American Literary Criticism from the Harlem Renaissance to the Present*, ed. Angelyn Mitchell (Durham, NC: Duke University Press, 1994), 170.

7. Fred Moten, *In the Break: The Aesthetics of the Black Radical Tradition* (Minneapolis: University of Minnesota Press, 2003), 90.

8. Ibid., Moten's emphasis.

9. Ibid., 91, Moten's emphasis.

10. Ibid., 92.

11. Ibid.

12. LeRoi Jones, *Blues People: Negro Music in White America* (Santa Barbara: Praeger, 1980).

13. LeRoi Jones, *Black Music* (London: Macgibbo & Kee, 1969).

14. Imamu Amiri Baraka, *The Music: Reflections on Jazz and Blues* (New York: William Morrow and Company, 1987).

15. Larry Neal, "The Black Arts Movement," 189.

16. Amiri Baraka, "Black Dada Nihilismus," in *The LeRoi Jones/Amiri Baraka Reader*, ed. William J. Harris (New York: Thundermouth, 1991), 71–73.

17. William J. Harris, "Introduction," in *The LeRoi Jones/Amiri Baraka Reader*, ed. William J. Harris (New York: Thundermouth, 1991), xxv.

18. Amiri Baraka, "Legacy," Poetry Foundation, accessed October 25, 2018.

19. Lucille Clifton, "my mama moved among the days," in *Good Times* (New York: Random House, 1969), 2.

20. Kathy Lou Schultz, "Amiri Baraka's 'Wise, Why's, Y's': Lineages of the Afro-Modernist Epic," *JML: Journal of Modern Literature* 35, no. 3 (2012): 25–50.

21. Jeffrey St. Onge and Jennifer Moore, "Poetry as a Form of Dissent: John F. Kennedy, Amiri Baraka, and the Politics of Art in Rhetorical Democracy," *Rhetoric Review* 35, no. 4 (2016): 335–47.

22. Ahad Mehrvand, "A Postcolonial Reading of Amiri Baraka's 21st Century Political Poem on America," *International Journal of Education and Literacy Studies* 4, no. 4 (2016): 21–29.

23. Ephraim Scott Sommers, "The Poem of Anger: Amiri Baraka, Tory Dent, and Adrian C. Louis," *Cream City Review* 40, no. 2 (2016): 40–63.

24. Patrick Roney, "The Paradox of Experience: Black Art and Black Idiom in the Work of Amiri Baraka," *African American Review* 37, no. 2/3 (2003): 417.

25. Roney, "The Paradox of Experience," 418–19.

26. Kathleen Grisham, "20th Century Art: Neo-Plasticism," Instructor Homepage, *West Valley College*, accessed October 25, 2018,

27. Gary Cox, *Existentialism and Excess: The Life and Times of Jean-Paul Sartre* (New York: Bloomsbury Academic, 2016), 224–26.

28. Cox, *Existentialism and Excess*, 224.

29. Amiri Baraka, "Reggae or Not," in *Transbluesency: Selected Poems* (New York: Marsilio, 1995), 175–85.

30. Saidiya V. Hartman, *Scenes of Subjection: Terror, Slavery, and Self-Making in Nineteenth-Century America* (New York: Oxford University Press, 1997).

31. Moten, *In the Break*, 4.

32. Moten, *In the Break*, 4.

33. Moten, *In the Break*, 91. Moten's emphasis.

34. William J. Harris, *The LeRoi Jones /Amiri Baraka Reader*, xxv.

35. Anne Fuchs, *A Space of Anxiety: Dislocation and Abjection in Modern German-Jewish Literature* (Atlanta: Rodopi, 1999), 1.

36. Rachel E. Harding, "Authority, History, and Everyday Mysticism in the Poetry of Lucille Clifton: A Womanist View," *Meridians: Feminism, Race, Transnationalism* 12, no. 1 (2014): 36–57.

37. Scarlett Cunningham, "The Limits of Celebration in Lucille Clifton's Poetry: Writing the Aging Woman's Body," *Frontiers: A Journal of Women Studies* 35, no. 2 (2014): 30–58.

38. Emilia Tetty Harjani, "The Feminist Voice in Lucille Clifton's 'The Thirty Eighth Year,' 'Miss Rosie' and 'Final Note to Clark.'" *Litera* 12, no. 1 (2013).

39. Mandolin Brassaw, "The Light That Came to Lucille Clifton: Beyond Lucille and Lucifer," *MELUS* 37, no. 3 (2012): 43–70.

40. Toi Derricotte, "Won't You Celebrate with Me: Remembering Lucille Clifton," *Callaloo* 33, no. 2 (2010): 373–79.

41. Lucille Clifton, "in the inner city," in *Good Times* (New York: Random House, 1969), 1.

42. Lucille Clifton, "my mama moved among the days," in *Good Times* (New York: Random House, 1969), 2.

43. Anne Fuchs, *A Space of Anxiety*, 1.

44. Lucille Clifton, "if something should happen," in *Good Times* (New York: Random House, 1969), 21.

Chapter Four

INTRODUCTION

The poets selected for the chapter devoted to Native American writers is not as concentrated on a particular time frame. This was due in part because of the writers and writing that I desired to discuss. Robin Coffee's poetry is a necessity in this study because of his speakers' devotion to engagement with historic traumas and their boisterous voice of empowerment. Peter Blue Cloud, whose poetry was published ten years earlier, was selected because of its focus on the Alcatraz occupation, but also because many of his poems engaged massive stressors and historical trauma, as well as the merging of present traumas within the speakers' lives and the manner in which the speaker recalled historic traumas in order to discuss massive stressors currently occurring within the speakers' lives. Like Coffee, Blue Cloud's poetry calls on the importance of cultural history in order to cope with present day distress. Finally, Linda Hogan was selected because of her poems' discussion of historic trauma, especially in the manner in which these historic traumas continue to influence the lives of her speakers. This is quite evident in her poem "The Truth Is" as the speaker attempts to cope with the legacy of trauma that exists not only as a historic trauma within the culture but one manifested in her speaker as she is both Native American and white.

As this study begins to examine the poetry of Native Americans, it is critical that we understand the significance that these poems have and what they are responding to politically. The poets I discuss in this chapter engage with historical traumas and do so in order to empower their culture and to demonstrate the universality of massive stressors that continue to impact Native Americans since the time of the Native American genocide. It is well documented that millions of Native Americans were killed, murdered, raped, enslaved, and displaced over hundreds of years. Given that our nation's history contains so many traumatic events that victimized Native Americans, it is no surprise that traces of historical trauma can still be found in poetry written by Native Americans in the second half of the twentieth century. Much like the previous chapter engaging African American poetry, the poetry examined in this chapter focuses more on historical trauma. This historic trauma has resulted in various psychological disorders that exist within individuals to this day, and statistical data focusing on substance abuse and psychological disorders within the Native American communities reinforce the idea that Native American history has shaped its future. According to an Indian Health Services study, Native Americans were 660 percent more likely to die of alcohol-related incidents, more than twice as likely to die of homicide, and 170 percent more likely to die of suicide than any other American race.[1] Such trauma is palpable within the poetry of various Native American poets such as Linda Hogan (Chickasaw), Peter Blue Cloud (Mohawk), and Robin Coffee (Cherokee/Creek/ Yankton Sioux), all of whom are discussed in the following chapter. These poets present images to be celebrated and that are unique to Native American culture in order to call for empowerment and to encourage community and nation building. Robin Coffee's poems uses the image of the warrior not only to show the violent and traumatic past of Native America, but to rejoice and celebrate the warrior as a powerfully symbolic figure of Native American culture. Peter Blue Cloud's poems present the importance of dance within Native American culture, as well as discussing the occupation of Alcatraz, which was intrinsic to the American Indian Movement. Finally, Linda Hogan's poems discuss the difficulties inherent in belonging to two different cultural traditions that have historically warred with one another. The speaker wishes to empower the Native American tradition, and, like the writing of other Native American poets, desires the empowerment and building of community for the people of her culture. Much like poets of the Black Arts Movement, the poets of this chapter work to build community and do so through a quest of empowerment by engaging historical trauma.

It would be beneficial to return to the ideas of Maria Yellow Horse Brave Heart, presented in the first chapter, as she is a scholar specializing in historical trauma theory as it pertains to Native Americans. Historical trauma, historical trauma response, and historically unresolved grief are important elements that must be kept within the forefront of a reader's mind when examining poetry through a literary trauma lens. Historical trauma theory attempts to fill the gaps left by the concept of post-traumatic stress disorder. Historical trauma theory transcends the surface-level diagnosis of PTSD to look back across generations in order to show how past atrocities inform the future and manifest themselves in subsequent generations in the form of abjection, isolation, unhomeliness, and revolutionary consciousness. Thus, historical trauma theory looks beyond surface, current causes to historical causes as the reasons for the negative symptoms found in today's cultural milieu surrounding the several groups focused on in the study. Brave Heart refers to previous studies she has published ("Gender Differences in the Historical Trauma Response among the Lakota" and "Oyate Ptayela: Rebuilding the Lakota Nation through Addressing Historical Trauma among Lakota Parents") and others (Robert W. Robin, Barbara Chester, and David Goldman's "Cumulative Trauma and PTSD in American Indian Communities") stating that historical trauma theory "describes massive cumulative trauma across generations rather than the more limited diagnosis of post-traumatic stress disorder (PTSD), which is inadequate for capturing the influence and characteristics of Native trauma."[2] PTSD fails to "adequately capture the influence and characteristics of Native trauma"[3] because PTSD usually pertains to situations in which a victim has experienced some sort of trauma firsthand, and it also does not account for the influences and characteristics of historical trauma present within Native American cultures and the poetry therein. Brave Heart's ideas merit mention here because the focus of her research is on trauma within Native American cultures and societies, thus her ideas are most aptly applied to the poetry of Native American writers. Although Brave Heart does advance our understanding of the poetry by allowing us a greater understanding of the concept of historical trauma, her ideas are insufficient in demonstrating how poems can explore and represent trauma in a way to redefine the culture and push for empowerment. Poems are able to unite through their words, and when exploring historical traumas and massive stressors that permeate a culture, the poems have the ability to move people, as has been witnessed in the art movements that ran parallel with political movements. Furthermore, when the political movement is not viewed as being representationally sufficient, as Clifton's poems did with the representation of women in the Black Arts Movement, the poetry can critique the movement as she did in her poem "my mama moved among the days."

The historical trauma that continues to permeate a culture, along with the racism that people of the culture may face, leads to more distress and debilitating behaviors. As Brave Heart articulates, the high rates of substance abuse, suicide, homicide, as well as oppression and poverty place Native Americans at a higher risk for trauma exposure. This is compounded as one considers the "background of historically traumatic losses across generations,"[4] which, according to Brave Heart, meet the criteria of genocide as defined by the United Nations. The lack of available resources, as is evident with many Native Americans, makes coping with both the immediate and historic trauma extremely difficult. As a result, the poetry of many Native

Americans, especially with the poems selected for this study, takes great care to articulate the unresolved grief which resides not only within the speaker of the poem but within the culture.

The writers of this chapter utilize poetry as a means to resist the long oppressive white culture that attempted to strip the culture from Native Americans by attempting to eliminate the language, art, values, and customs in order to Europeanize the various nations of Native America. As such, the poets are engaging with trauma in order to unite the people of the culture and empower the people. Each speaker in this section uses their voice as a form of resistance to this oppression through the language of the oppressor. Although some poets attempt to break the bounds of the oppressor's language by writing in their language, this falls beyond the scope of this study. Likewise, some poets like Jerome Rothenberg focus on the use of oral poetics, which is again working against the oppressor by focusing on the traditional oral art rather than written language, and this also falls outside the focus of this study but would be a beneficial study worth pursuing. The poets of this chapter focus a great deal on imagery that is unique and important to Native American culture. Many of the poems interject these images, like that of the warrior or ceremonial dance, around images that are more universal. Unlike the poetry of the previous chapter, where poets of the Black Arts Movement fought to establish a unique black perspective and unique black art, the poets of this chapter fight against the oppressor by fighting within it. The Native American poems of this chapter do not try as hard to separate their culture from the oppressive white culture but try instead to carve out a segment within the oppressive culture.

What this creates is a sense of ambivalence; the voices appear to want to break away by placing highly cultural significant images within the poem, but elements and images of the white oppressor are still resonant within the poetry. Ambivalence also resides, as discussed earlier, in the production of poetry from resistance against the oppressor, yet the poetry is written in English, which is the voice of the oppressor, and presented in a written form, which is not the traditional form of Native American poetry. Finally, ambivalence resides in how the resistance is partially a call to fight while also very nomadic, thus attempting to get away. In the following, the poetry of Coffee, Blue Cloud, and Hogan will be examined through a literary trauma lens focusing on abjection, isolation, unhomeliness, ambivalence, and traumatic figurative language. Much like the poetry of African Americans and Japanese Americans discussed earlier, these poems illustrate these characteristics as a result of a speaker's historic trauma response as a result of unresolved historic trauma. Coffee's poetry is filled with anger, hostility, and is quite similar to the poetry of Amiri Baraka in its angry tone. Much of his subject matter engages historical traumas of the past and his speaker's attempt to engage these horrors of the past. In Hogan's poetry, the speaker grapples with double consciousness influenced by the fact that the speaker's family is composed of whites and Native Americans, and the internal struggle that exists as she engages historical trauma. Her poetry also speaks a great deal on abjection and unhomeliness. Finally, Blue Cloud's poetry discusses abjection and isolation as the speaker compares his existence, and the existence of other Native Americans, to an island, and more specifically, the island of Alcatraz. What is ultimately produced by the poets is a call for empowerment and national formation as the speakers engage with historic traumas that continue to inflict massive stressors into the lives of people today. By discussing events that occurred and the cultural traditions, the poems are encouraging Native Americans to establish artistic and political movements to advance Native America.

ABJECTION AND UNHOMELINESS IN THE POETRY OF ROBIN COFFEE

Outside of a rather superficial book review, nothing has been written on the poetry of Robin Coffee. Coffee never rose to the prominence of the other poets of this study, but his poetry is an excellent example of historical trauma manifest within an individual that is articulated in verse. In Coffee's collection *A Scar upon Our Voice*, there are many poems that exhibit abjection and unhomeliness, such as "Loneliness," "Lonely Gifted Traveler," "Touched by a Little Sadness," and "My Place beyond Sadness." Each of these poems discusses wandering and, at times, a nomadic existence where the speaker discusses the desire or need for movement, which is often accompanied by sadness. The speakers in these poems also discuss the isolation they confront and the wandering in search for community.

This abjection is clearly articulated in Coffee's poem "Voices in the Water,"[5] where the speaker not only wanders but also discusses the pain of isolation, even when spending time with another. In the poem, we find the speaker riding in a bus with no specific destination in mind. While traveling, he meets another person also traveling for the sake of travel, and they discuss the difficulties of being strangers on their own land. The beginning of the poem discusses the speaker's meeting an individual named Buffalohead (line 2) and their sharing in both conversation and a bottle of wine "We only just met / His name was Buffalohead / We split a bottle of wine" (lines 1–3). The fact that the speaker has met someone on a bus and is able to form a bond with him so quickly (giving their willingness to share a bottle of wine) is quite strange, yet the fact that Buffalohead was also Native American gives insight into the idea that although they may be complete strangers, they share the common bond of being Native American and may be able to understand similar difficulties. By the third line, the two are already sharing a bottle of wine, which indicates the significance that the substance has to both men. The two men are playing into the stereotype of Native Americans and alcohol, which is not unfounded given the statistics about alcoholism presented earlier. The wine is significant, as has been discussed in earlier chapters, as it is symbolic of the ability to flee, as drugs and alcohol provide a certain type of flight. The speaker tells how Buffalohead refers to the wine as water that can be used to extinguish a fire that is a presumable one that each of them associate with the struggles of their lives: "He called it water / To douse / A life's fire" (lines 4–6). Buffalohead is telling the speaker he is using the alcohol precisely for this reason—as an escape from the traumas of life, which is his "life's fire."

The lack of punctuation, although very common within Coffee's poetry, does not create a great deal of confusion, but the lack of punctuation coupled with the short lines and lack of any stanza breaks forces the images and narrative of the poem to progress quickly, which could be indicative of the speed with which the two men began to know each other, but also the quickness by which they were able to share intimate aspects of their lives. The entire narrative unfolds very quickly, from the friendship starting in the first two lines, the shared alcohol by the third line, to the conversation of being lonely in the tenth line.

Abjection becomes more evident in the lines that follow as the speaker discusses the feeling of isolation they both share: "We talked / Of being alone / In the city" (lines 7–9.) The next lines reinforce this idea as the speaker discusses aimlessly wandering about the city in a bus with "Nowhere to go / No on to go to" (lines 10–11). The isolation, which both individuals in the poem discuss, is important because it demonstrates neither person has a place where he feels at home or a community to be emotionally supportive. Both men suggest they have nowhere to go to and no one to visit. The travel the two are undertaking is not to a particular locale but travel for travel's sake as stated in the next lines:

> He was going somewhere
> On faith alone he said
> I was going somewhere
> Alone with my faith (lines 12–15)

Buffalohead's travel is "On faith alone" (line 13), thus he is traveling with the belief that he will be taken care of along the way. The speaker, however, is traveling alone with only his beliefs, as the simple changing of the word order of the lines demonstrate (line 15). The difference is subtle, but important, in that each traveler possesses a feeling of isolation even when traveling with someone with whom he shares much in common.

The poem continues as the speaker states that he is unable to see Buffalohead's face, "We rode the bus / I could not see his face" (lines 16–17). As such, the reader is presented with an individual stripped of his identity as he travels, which is reinforced by the fact the speaker is never given a gender, much less an identity. This stripping of identity is as the poem concludes by making both speakers voices in the water:

> Tonight he said
>   We are
> Voices in the water
> Strangers in our land
> The night becomes a blur. (lines 18–22)

The poem concludes by presenting two individuals without identity and traveling with no particular destination; they exist in a state of abjection, and, as line 21 suggests, they are both "Strangers in our land" (line 18) with voices in the wine the two are drinking (lines 18–21). With this, the identities of the two are stripped again, becoming only voices. Given that Buffalohead refers to the wine spoken of earlier in the poem as water, it is logical to reason that this reference to water is another reference to alcohol, thus making the two not just voices, but voices within the alcohol. This renders their existence not only fleeting in the sense of a voice, but without substance since it exists only through intoxication. However, one should not discount the importance that water has played in the past to Native American cultures. Many creation stories involve water, and water has ties to spirituality. Perhaps more realistically, water is one of the most precious substances on the planet. Many nations and settlings, in the Americas and beyond, were founded around easily accessible water sources. Therefore, the speaker and Buffalohead are the voices that people of their culture *need*, even though they are strangers in their own land. The speaker and Buffalohead are searching, as their ancestors may have, for a home. This is a type of resistance as the two search for a place to reside outside the reach of the dominant white culture and is a call for others to establish a different culture. The voices are a means of expression, which is vital to a culture's existence, thus the speaker and Buffalohead are wandering in search for a means of expression outside the white culture.

The feeling of abjection and unhomeliness reaches its zenith in the poem as the speaker described the two travelers as "Strangers in our land" (line 21), giving the two a complete feeling of unhomeliness. They not only have nowhere to go and no one to go to, but they are left as strangers in a land that was once their home. This sense of unhomeliness is the result of historical trauma still affecting the speaker and Buffalohead, to the point that, in this moment, they exist only in the abject state. The final line of the poem concludes the poem not in a resolution, but in a fading out that leaves the poem as only a fragment in the lives of these individuals with no real background or conclusion to their existence (line 22).

As can be seen in this example, poems such as "Voices in the Water" articulate struggle and do so in an ambivalent manner where they are attempting to resist the white culture, but as they resist, they also remain within it. Buffalohead and the speaker are fleeing, but doing so in a means of public transport, which is owned by the same white government that inflicted the historical trauma upon their culture. The poem resists and attempts to become a voice, but that voice uses that oppressor's language. Buffalohead calls the water wine, which creates another ambivalent dynamic; water is essential for life, but in this instance, alcohol is referred to as water. Alcohol exists, in the poem, as a type of *pharmakon*; it is a substance that is necessary for life (water), but also the substance that causes destruction (alcohol). In addition, the poem demonstrates many aspects inherent to poetry representing trauma. Unlike most short stories or novels, the reader is left with only this fragment of information about the speaker and Buffalohead. Like the fragmented existence that is often felt by survivors of trauma, the poem resides permanently in this fragmented state. This is a substantial reason why poetry is a strong medium for presenting trauma. Poetry not only utilizes images, which is often how traumatic memories exist, but the poem is fragmented, much like the traumatic memories; therefore, poetry can be a very strong representation of how the speaker may feel and understand the world. In addition to presenting trauma within his poems using abjection and unhomeliness, the speakers in Coffee's poems also present traumatic figurative language, as the next section will demonstrate.

One of the most intriguing elements of Coffee's poetry, and which continues to be presented by Blue Cloud and Hogan, is the ambivalence that exists within the poetry. The ambivalence in the poetry embodies elements of uncertainty in how to establish a new form of nation-building, uncertainty in the future for Native Americans, disorientation associated with trauma, and the need for empowerment and nation-building. It is important to note as the study continues discussing these selections of Native American poetry, ambivalence is a reoccurring characteristic with the poems spanning several decades. This ambivalence demonstrates an uncertainty in how to establish a culture outside of the white culture since the white culture has become so oppressive and destroyed so much of the Native American culture. Although it is quite apparent that there is a distinct Native American culture, certain aspects, like the English language and written language, as well as modern medicines and cities, have permeated Native American culture and forever changed it. As such, trying to establish a uniquely Native American culture is very difficult given the influence that white culture has had on Native America for so many years. Furthermore, returning to the original Native American culture also means having to face a painful traumatic history.

This ambivalence, as it exists in trying to establish a new Native American culture, also creates anxieties about the future of the culture. As the white influence continues to affect the Native American culture and change it, this influence could eventually destroy or overtake the culture. As such, there is a *need* to establish a strong Native American culture that fights against the white oppressor, allows for a political movement and an arts movement to preserve Native American culture and tradition. This ambivalence, and the uncertainty that it provokes, can be used to encourage the readers to take steps to preserve and empower Native American culture and politics. As a result of the ambivalence present with the poems, it also creates a disorienting feel that is synonymous with the effect of massive stressors and traumatic stressors.

ROBIN COFFEE AND THE WARRIOR

In the poetry of Coffee's *A Scar upon Our Voice*,[6] the most prominent traumatic metaphor is the speaker of the poems presenting himself as a warrior in the same vein as the Native Americans of hundreds of years ago who fought against colonization by Europeans. In poems such as "In from the Cold,"[7] "No Other Way,"[8] and "Warriors of This Time,"[9] the speaker presents himself as a warrior set to fight. In the poem "In from the Cold," for example, the speaker instructs another to fight against the system set up to oppress his people. The metaphor compares the fight his people must now take to the fight of warriors from hundreds of years ago. Another instance occurs in the poem "Blood of a Warrior,"[10] as the speaker discusses how the blood that runs through his veins is the same as his ancestors who fought many battles against white oppression and colonialism. The speaker states that his blood is ready to continue this fight, even though, like his ancestors, his people are outnumbered. Again, there is ambivalence within the voice of the speaker as he attempts to empower his people by calling them to arms to become warriors, but acknowledges that they are again outnumbered, and will most likely be defeated, thereby disempowering his people again. Even though the speaker is well aware of the obstacle that he faces, and the inevitable defeat, he pushes forward and calls his brethren to do the same in their resistance.

The speakers of Coffee's poems use the image of the warrior as the speaker engages the racism, massive stressors, and trauma incurred by Native

Americans for generations. Even though the speakers of Coffee's poems use this powerful image of the warrior to encourage empowerment against oppression, there are still elements of ambivalence residing within the poem. In order to discuss historic trauma and empowerment, it is no surprise that his poem "Blood of a Warrior" begins by calling upon the speaker's ancestors who survived many battles. The poem begins by stating:

> Through my veins
> Old blood runs
> Alive having survived
> Many battlegrounds. (lines 1–4)

This is significant because it demonstrates how the speaker is utilizing traumatic figurative language and is calling upon historic trauma, which still affects him. The traumatic figurative language resides in the idea that the blood that runs in his veins is the same blood that existed in those that fought in battle. This idea is generated by calling the blood "old," and suggesting it endured many battles (lines 3–4). The metaphor does not become complete until the end of the poem.

The speaker is also using the warrior and the warrior's blood as a call for resistance. The warriors of history refused to accept the suffering and oppression that was forced upon them. Native Americans were notorious for fighting against whites and, as Howard Zinn notes in *The People's History of the United States*, whites often abandoned the idea of enslaving Native Americans because of their staunch resistance.[11] The poem continues by telling how the blood just spoken of screams against the false promises made in the past:

> It raises its voice
> Against
> The illusion of freedom
> In a promised land. (lines 5–8)

These lines are an absolute call of resistance to the legacy that historic trauma has left behind for people to engage with. Rather than accept the false promises of freedom (line 7), the speaker's very own blood resists the treatment of his people. The raising of his voice in line 5 is the first instance of raising that exists three different times in the poem. The second instance appears in line 9 as the speaker states, "It raises its voice / Against injustice for all / Amber waves of pain" (lines 9–11). In lines 5 and 9, the blood raises its voice against injustices, and in line 14, the heart of the speaker rises as a response to the blood's voice. The repetition of this rising draws attention this movement, which is an act of resistance throughout the poem.

The poem concludes by discussing the idea of engaging with the oppression and trauma directly, as it states:

> The voice of warrior-blood
> Stirs my heart
> To rise and stand
> Like
> 30 warriors
> Against
> 200 cavalrymen. (lines 12–18)

The speaker is facing historic trauma and engaging this legacy head on and doing so, not through historically unresolved grief but historically unresolved anger. The speaker resists not just because he desires a better way of life, but also because he is called to by the very blood in his veins, which is a blood of warriors that refused to accept defeat, disrespect, oppression, or suffering.

This type of resistance is especially significant because it is responding to trauma in a manner unique to Native Americans. The resistance is specific in how it takes the form of a call toward warrior militancy and does so by incorporating the historic resistance and culture of Native America. This technique calls for resistance by means of art and language, two things that the oppressors tried to strip from the Native Americans. As such, the speaker shows that the current and historical injustices have affected Native Americans, as is evident by the language being used, but the will to fight, even centuries later, is still strong. The poem establishes that these are actually both current and historic injustices.

This is perhaps best illustrated in lines 10 and 11, "Against injustice for all / Amber waves of pain." The tenth line is a play on a line from the American Pledge of Allegiance, and the eleventh is an obvious allusion to the famous lyrics of "American the Beautiful." By changing the words in this manner, the speaker is able to illustrate the vastly different and trauma-filled history of Native Americans, while also demonstrating how some of the trauma is still reverberating in the culture. By adding the word "against" and using a homophonic play on words from the American Pledge of Allegiance, the speaker is able to suggest that injustice was used against all Native Americans. Additionally, by using a well-known American patriotic (or propaganda) song, the speaker is able to show that the happiness and pride many Americans may feel came at the cost of his people. Furthermore, by replacing the word "grain" with "pain," which maintains the same rhyme in order to be more apparent, the pain appears, not only widespread, as grain is in this nation, but also suggests it was purposefully planted.

The urge to resist is shown in the final lines of the poem where the speaker feels the need to fight against the injustices like warriors who were greatly outnumbered by the U. S. cavalry (lines 12–18). These lines complete the metaphor, as the blood, which has been spoken of in the poem, is shown to be warrior-blood (line 12) of a Native American, and thus the speaker is comparing the current inequalities and oppression to the atrocities that occurred to Native Americans in the past as well as the bloodshed as a result of battles and wars. Although this idea is presented in the title, it is not until the image of the last three lines that the significance of the blood becomes apparent. The speaker desires to fight the oppression in the same manner as his ancestors but understands the great disadvantage as articulated in the last three lines.

The idea that current oppression and inequality are related to historic trauma is tangible within the poem, so the metaphor is able to show the despair, anger, and frustration that the speaker has against the inequalities, but the imagery also harkens to the historic traumas of the past. The fact that the speaker is using the metaphor for a warrior is unique to his culture, and the resistance that he calls on, even though it is against nearly insurmountable odds, is similar to the fights his ancestors fought. There is a play of ambivalence in this call to resistance because, although the speaker is calling for his brethren to resist the oppression and fight back, he acknowledges in this metaphor that the fights will most likely result in defeat. The odds are not only clearly against the warriors, but being so highly outnumbered, the idea of winning appears impossible. This is highlighted as lines 16 and 18 begin with digits. As such, they standout, not only by their placement at the beginning of the line but also by being digits rather than being spelled out.

The poem is structured with very short lines, the longest being four words, so the reader's eyes are forced quickly down the page. In addition, the poem contains no stanza breaks, so the reader is forced to encounter the entire poem without a rest. This technique forces the reader to feel rushed as she reads down the page, and the line breaks in these short lines force the reader to focus on certain words and phrases. The use of violent imagery, such as "blood" (line 2) and "battlegrounds" (line 4), creates a sense of violence while, in the sixth and seventeenth lines, the word "against" resides alone, forcing the reader to pay special attention to the word. Because of the lack of punctuation and stanza breaks, the poem becomes confusing and disorienting. This feeling forces the reader to reread certain sections in order to make sense out of the poem, just as the mind attempts to reevaluate traumatic events in order to gain a greater understanding. These techniques are not readily available in prose writing; thus, by presenting this idea in a poem, the speaker is able to create feelings and ideas that may not be as easily presented in a short story or novel.

Many of Coffee's poems are composed of short lines, and these often contain few or no stanza breaks. Presenting poems in this manner creates a sense of urgency, which is appropriate for the majority of Coffee's poems and subject matter. This urgency is appropriate because many of Coffee's speakers are calling for action and empowerment. The urgency creates the sense that changes must be made, and people must fight against the oppressor before they are wiped out. This creates a feeling of uneasiness that amplifies the urgency further. Furthermore, the uneasy feeling this creates is reinforced by the fact that many of the pages of *A Scar upon Our Voice* share more than one poem per page, and the poems are forced to share space with other poems, which may or may not be related in subject matter. This is a very important and appropriate technique given the history of reservations and displacement in Native America, and this format would not be feasible for poems with longer lines. Peter Blue Cloud also presents many of his poems with short lines, but he allows the poems to reside on their own page, unlike Coffee. Because of the repetition of traumatic figurative language used in some of Blue Cloud's poems, along with the technique of placing multiple poems on the same page would not have been appropriate.

Coffee's poems engage traumatic history in their subject matter but also do so using traumatic figurative language, abjection, and unhomeliness. The speakers in these poems encourage resistance against the dominant white oppression that originated centuries before and continues to this day. The poetic resistance created here is unique in its use of the warrior image and the undaunted manner in which the warriors fought against the oppressors throughout history. The speaker also demonstrates a play of ambivalences, another aspect unique to Native American trauma poetry compared to the poetry of the African Americans and Japanese Americans. The ambivalence in "Voices in the Water" resides in the play with water and alcohol. The speaker refers to the wine, highly significant due to the extremely high levels of alcoholism and stereotypes in the Native American community, with water, an essential part of life for an individual and community. Alcohol, for some, is the reason for living and something that is depended on, while also being the cause of destruction and death for thousands. Equally significant is the manner in which the speaker of other Coffee poems calls for resistance through the metaphor and image of the warrior, yet also hints at the inevitable defeat. The call for resistance is part of a warrior spirit that refuses to die yet is unable to win. Similar calls for resistance and ambivalence reside in the poems of Peter Blue Cloud and Linda Hogan. These calls for resistance are also mixed with traumatic figurative language, abjection, and unhomeliness, just as the poetry of Coffee due to the historical trauma that resides within the Native American culture. In the poetry of Blue Cloud, this desire to establish power for the Native American culture is palpable, especially when considering the proximity that Blue Cloud's poems were written, especially in subject matter, to the American Indian Movement.

PETER BLUE CLOUD: RECLAIMING ALCATRAZ

The second poet selected for this chapter is Peter Blue Cloud, who was selected not only because he is a preeminent Native American poet (Mohawk), his calls for resistance to the oppression plaguing Native Americans, but also because he represents trauma and isolation in his poems about Alcatraz. Unlike the trauma metaphor used by the speakers in poems by Coffee, which compares the current oppression against Native Americans to the battles of the past, the speakers in Blue Cloud's poems repeatedly state that every tribe is an island in his poem "Alcatraz,"[12] which creates many levels of meaning given the history of that particular island. Alcatraz is most commonly known as a former federal prison, but before this it was used as a military prison for Civil War soldiers.[13] Most importantly, between 1969 and 1971, Native American groups occupied Alcatraz three different times, with the most famous occupation beginning on November 9, 1969.[14] The occupation of Alcatraz was a major catalyst for what became known as the American Indian Movement. Richard Oakes planned the occupation for himself and a group of Native American students, and it lasted for nineteen months. According to the U.S. National Parks Service website, Oakes and the students "claimed the island in the name of Indians of all tribes."[15] The island, therefore, has cultural significance for Native Americans in this regard, but the island also acts as a subject for traumatic figurative language in Blue Cloud's poems. The idea of using the former prison island as the basis for these poems is, like Coffee, a call for resistance as well as a play with ambivalence. The island was occupied, which was an act of resistance, and to write about the island is to celebrate the event. However, the island, while a move toward freedom for Native Americans, is also the site of American incarceration. Furthermore, what is being fought for and prized is the abandoned island used for the incarceration of the worst criminals.

Little has been written about the poetry of Peter Blue Cloud, which is unfortunate given Blue Cloud's strength as a poet, his history as a political activist, and the manner in which he is able to discuss trauma within his poetry. The first of Blue Cloud's poems to be examined here is aptly entitled "Alcatraz," blending contemporary imagery like the Golden Gate Bridge with images of Native Americans dancing. The focus of the poem is the idea that a tribe is an island, which is repeated in several lines throughout the poem.

The image of an island is most significant when considering the island that is presented in the title. In the poem, Alcatraz exists as a metaphor for the unhomeliness Native Americans faced by means of reservations, which acted more or less as prisons. The speaker makes this known beginning on line 6, where she states, "and a tribe is an island, and a tribe is an island." This is repeated in lines 11 and 12 and lastly on line 14, with only small changes. With the island referred to in the title being Alcatraz and with the repetition of a tribe being an island, the speaker is able to suggest the idea of Native American historical treatment and the relegation of Native Americans to reservations. The tribe as an island repeats in these poems, and thus the tribe is cut off and imprisoned by both physical means from the past and from the past itself. Just as the reservations acted as a type of imprisonment, the destruction of cultural heritage by the United States government and religious zealots made impossible the preservation of culture, which was especially destructive given that most Native American history was preserved orally. As a result, many Native Americans are cut off from a portion of their cultural heritage and exist as an island.

The event that is being celebrated was also an act of revolutionary resistance as many Native Americans took steps to demand equality and Indian rights. The first one occurred in 1964 and the second one November 9, 1969, which was eleven days before the third. The third, and most recognized occupation, lasted nineteen months and spanned from November 20, 1969, until 1972.[16] Troy Johnson notes in his article "The Occupation of Alcatraz Island: Root of American Indian Activism" that, as a result of the occupations of Alcatraz (there were three total, spanning from 1969 to 1972), the number of bills passed by Congress went up substantially, from six of the twenty-two proposed in the 91st Congress to forty-six being passed during the 92nd Congress.[17] Furthermore, Johnson states, "President Nixon increased the budget of the BIA by 224 percent, doubled the funds for Indian health, established the first special Office of Indian Water Rights, and made special provisions for presenting to any federal court the trustee's position defending Indian natural resources rights."[18] Johnson reminds us that credit should not be given fully to the American Indian Movement,[19] for, as mentioned earlier, the occupation that ended in 1972 was the third occupation, although it was the longest and most recognized.[20] The first occupation occurred four years before the American Indian Movement was even founded, as Lee Irwin writes, "In 1968, George Mitchell and Dennis Banks (Chippewas) founded AIM in Minneapolis in an attempt to force better treatment for inner-city Native peoples harassed constantly by police and other city officials."[21] Not long after Banks and Mitchell formed AIM, "Clyde and Vernon Bellecourt (Chippewa) and Russell Means (Oglala) joined AIM and, in 1969, AIM members joined with other Native peoples in the occupation of Alcatraz Island."[22] About the occupation, Stephan Cornell identifies the event as "a watershed. It drew massive publicity, provided many Indians with a dramatic symbol of self-assertion."[23] Johnson furthers this idea as he states, "More importantly for young Indian people, the occupation of Alcatraz Island became the springboard for the rise of Indian activism beginning in 1969 and continuing into the late 1970s, as witnessed by the large number of occupations which began shortly after the November 20, 1969 landing."[24] The American Indian Movement, and other activism performed by Native Americans, was unique in how it pushed for inclusion within the United States, especially legally, yet the movement also wanted to retain a type of cultural identity. This idea, akin to the Black Arts Movement, is somewhat ambivalent itself in that it desired to be included and excluded at the same time. Therefore, it may not be of such great surprise to see the desire for resistance in the poetry of Native Americans, while also containing elements of ambivalence. As such, an island is a perfect metaphor for the American Indian Movement, as an island, when part of a country, is both part of the nation but also separate onto itself.

The poem beings by stating, "As lightning strikes the Golden Gate / and fire dances the city streets" (lines 1–2). Allusions to the past are presented in the poem in the form of dance, which is also repeated throughout the poem. By bringing the Golden Gate Bridge and city streets into the first two lines, the reader is given an indication that the setting of the poem is modern. By mixing dancing with modern imagery, the speaker is able to call on cultural history and place it in the present. The streets and the bridge are being attacked by nature in these lines as the Golden Gate Bridge is said to have been struck by lightning in the first line and fire is said to be dancing in the streets in the second line. Nature attacking manmade structures would be a reversal of what occurred during colonization, so presenting these images is a call to overturn colonialism and the devastation and trauma brought to the Native Americans. This call for overturning the "white man's world" is symbolic for the many political actions occurring both in California (Alcatraz) and in Washington, D.C.

The people in the poem are given strong cultural identification as to which Nation they belong to, yet their sexes and names are never revealed. This is significant because it allows the people within the poem to represent nearly anyone belonging to the cultural group. Identity is manifested there and nowhere else, other than the Navajo being a child. What is evident, other than which Indian Nation they belong to, is the elements of sadness, which each of the people in the poem exhibits. The poem continues by stating, "a Navajo child whimpers the tide's pull / and Sioux and Cheyenne dance lowly to the ground" (lines 3–4). The Navajo child is whimpering "the tide's pull" (line

3), and this is important considering a tribe is an island, which is repeated throughout the poem. The tide, therefore, reinforces the isolation felt, and the dance performed by the other people performed lowly (line 4). The Navajo child feels a contradictory pull that is placed on many to conform to white society or to cling to the cultural beliefs that reside within the Nation, which is quite similar to DuBois's idea of double consciousness. The strong tide, as it pulls on the island of Alcatraz in San Francisco Bay in an opposing direction every few hours, could be likened to the confusion that resides in identity, especially as the poem repeats a tribe is an island.

It must be noted that many Native American dances are performed low to the ground; however, one cannot dismiss the significance of the word lowly considering the whimpering child and traumatic figurative language being used in this poem. The fact that they are dancing is incredibly important to Native American culture because of the important role that dance plays. The dancing allows for a means of expression, just like the art presented during the Black Arts Movement, which was unique to the specific culture and resided outside the Eurocentric scope of art recognized by white America. The fact that people of many Native American Nations are dancing together is highly significant because it signifies a newfound unity that was not as pronounced in the past. This is a united front against the oppression that each nation has faced in the past and continues to face today. The people of the Nations are connected, not only because of this cause and similar cultures and histories, but through a common trauma. These poems engage massive stressors and trauma by using traumatic figurative language, but do so in a manner that is indirect, suggesting that Native American culture has been othered, or placed lower in the cultural hierarchy of the dominant culture—that is, white. The speaker of other poems by Blue Cloud engage trauma more directly, yet they still utilize traumatic figurative language.

The second stanza of this poem begins with one of the most interesting lines of the poem: "Tomorrow is breathing my shadow's heart" (line 5). The stanza continues, "and a tribe is an island, and a tribe is an island, / and silhouettes are the Katchina dancers / of my beautiful people." (6–8). The fifth line is rather enigmatic when read at first gland, but the line becomes clearer when associated with the "Katchina dancers" (line 7) mentioned a few lines later. The Katchina are very significant in that

> They are associated with the ancestral dead and with duties such as bringing rain. In Hopi mythology they live in the San Francisco Mountains (which is also the location of the world of the dead) and their return from there to the people is symbolized in dances, where male dancers dress in masks and costumes, each designed to represent an individual kachina. The masked dancers take on

the powers of the kachinas during the dance, and the masks must not be worn outside the ceremony.[25]

The Katchina dancers mentioned in the poem are said to be the "silhouettes" (line 7) of the various Native Americans mentioned before. Thus, not only is the placement of the poem, San Francisco, very significant, but the dancers are also very important because "the being depicted through the regalia is thought to be actually present with the performer, temporarily transforming him."[26] These dancers lose their identity, much as the other Native Americans mentioned in the poem, and the people whom they represent are dead ancestors. Therefore, returning to the first line of the stanza, the "shadow's heart" (line 5) represents the historical trauma that still resonated in tomorrow's breath. The repetition of trauma is represented not only in the first line but symbolically in the Katchina dancers, as well. These images buttress the repeated idea that a tribe is an island. In fact, the rhythm and repetition in line 6, "and a tribe is an island, and a tribe is an island," adds the image of the Katchina dancing through the rhythm as it is read. The idea of a tribe being an island takes on even more significance as it is understood that the Katchina are able to bring rain.

Not only are the Katchina able to bring rain, but this is also a trait said to belong to Coyote, who is mentioned in the very last line of the poem. The idea of rain is important for two different facets of the poem. Not only could the bringing of rain potentially generate an island, but the lightning that has struck the Golden Gate Bridge early in the poem could also be related to the Katchina and Coyote. Likewise, the fire that is said to be dancing in the streets could be extinguished if rain did occur. As such, the Katchina and possibly Coyote could be responsible for the lightning, which is attacking modern culture, and the lack of rain could be allowing the fire to consume the city streets. Each of these could be the result of the people said to be dancing lowly in the first stanza.

The idea of a tribe being an island is repeated in the third stanza but does not appear until the last two lines of the third stanza. The rhythm, however, is spoken of in the first two lines, as the poem states, "Heart and heaven and spirit / written in a drum's life cycle" (lines 9–10). The rhythm of these lines is different from line 6, but the reference to the drum is important to the dance, which is nearly always present in Native Americans' songs connected to dance. The inclusion of heart in line 9 is perhaps more significant to any other rhythm of the poem. Just as each tribe is an island, each person carries inside them their own beat through their heart, and by using two trochaic words to follow heart ("spirit" and "heaven"), the sound mimics a heartbeat and allows for a pause between by using unstressed ands. This heart, as well

Chapter Four

as the spirit and heaven, is written in the life cycle of the drum, and this drum is creating the beat that the people are dancing to earlier on. Consequently, the dance of the people is being mediated by the beat that is related to the historical trauma manifested in the heart.

The stanza concludes by repeating a variation of line 6 by stating, "and a tribe is an island, forever, / forever we have been an island" (lines 11–12). These lines are similar to line 6, yet the separation that exists by splitting lines 11 and 12, so as to less mirror line 6, is very significant. Each island, in lines 11 and 12, is isolated, much the overall theme of isolation that exists within the poem. However, the "we" and "tribe" is a collective that exists in isolation, which creates a feeling of ambivalence in the idea of being both isolated yet in a group that is isolated. By placing the word "forever" on the end of line 11 and beginning of line 12 draws attention to the idea that this collective isolation is very permanent, drawing attention again to the juxtaposition of new images (Golden Gate) and harkening back to older traditions of dance and demonstrating the changes that have occurred.

The final stanza of the poem begins with the line, "As we sleep our dreaming in eagles," (line 13). If a comma had been placed between "sleep" and "our," this line could be understood to mean that as the people sleep, their dreams could have been of eagles and even dreaming that they were eagles. However, no comma exists here, yet one does exist at the end of this line and others with in the poem. Therefore, this prevents this line from being read in such a way. Thus, when read closer, the word "dreaming" changes from a verb to a noun so that they are sleeping their dreams, which means resting upon one's dreams or taking a break from dreaming. The dreaming that was occurring was "in eagles," which, given the animals' ability to fly, represents freedom, which is also symbolic for freedom in American national symbolism. This should not be lost on the reader. The hypersymbolism of the eagle, within American symbolism, is presented in a poem about the taking away of freedoms from people who first resided in the land now occupied by the United States.

As the final stanza continues, the repeated phrase "a tribe is an island" occurs again in line 14. The isolation presented here refers to the previous line as the speaker discusses the idea of putting both freedom and dreams on hold, but the line is followed by a similar line "and a tribe is a people" (line 15), which not only deviates from the repetition from earlier within the poem, but reminds the reader of the humanity of Native Americans that was often ignored or disputed in the past. By placing the idea that "a tribe is a people" (line 15) here, the speaker is also pushing the reader to focus on the treatment of Native Americans, in the past and present, as well as the idea of freedom and lack thereof. However, this line also needs to be read with the final line of the poem. Together, the final three lines read "a tribe is an island / and a tribe is a people / in the eternity of Coyote's mountain" (14–16). It is well established that Coyote is a trickster character within many different Native American cultures. Coyote mountain is an actual mountain with the Anza-Borrego Desert State Park, but I do not think the speaker is referring to this mountain. Close to San Francisco is the Coyote Hills Regional Park, which was originally inhabited by the Ohlone Indians, but became dedicated as a public park in 1967.[27] Therefore, in 1967, land that was once used by Native Americans became land reserved for all people to access, for a fee, and belongs to the government. Thus, the land belonged both to no one and everyone. Furthermore, this occurred during the Native American Alcatraz occupation when a group of Native Americans were trying to take back government land and claim it for Native Americans. Presenting this idea in this manner, and the idea of taking back the island, is very Coyote-like. By closing the poem like this, the speaker is presenting the idea that all Native Americans need to work together regardless of their "tribe" as indicated on line 15, but it also suggests that in order to gain land and power back from the U.S. government, people may have to use Coyote-like tactics, like the Occupation of Alcatraz.

Blue Cloud's speaker discusses trauma more directly in his poem "For Ace,"[28] but the speaker still utilizes traumatic figurative language in order to discuss the pain of losing a friend. In "For Ace," the speaker discusses the death of a friend and tells how the death is both a loss for him and the world. He recounts parts of his friend's life, but he focuses on Ace's painting. The speaker is brought into one of Ace's paintings where he is forced to confront his culture's traumatic past. Much longer than Blue Cloud's poem "Alcatraz," "For Ace" begins with the speaker discussing sadness:

> I cannot summon a tear
> or feel badly just now,
> it's not my loss so much
> as it is all our losing. (lines 1–4)

It is evident, even here, that the speaker is moving the feeling of sadness and loss beyond his own personal loss and into the public sphere. The speaker is able to make this movement by stating that he cannot feel bad because the loss is more than just personal; it is a loss for everyone.

The second stanza discusses how there will not be any of the traditional type of ceremonies or actions that would have been done in the past:

> There won't be a journey to
> the pueblo where he was born
> or any tracings of childhood

> there in red clay dust where
> he might have sketched pictures
> with a twig, (lines 5–10)

This moves the idea of the poem into a contemporary space, and it also demonstrates the loss of culture that may have been the result of Ace's actions. The discussion of Ace's sketches in the red dust also act as a foreshadowing of his abilities as an artist. However, the fact that it was done in dust also demonstrates the impermanence of life and childhood. The third stanza states that there will not be anger at his being taken away, in death, like the many others were taken away from their families by the government to be sent to government schools:

> and no anger at his being taken
> from family and home, away
> to government school like
> so many others. (lines 11–14)

This turn is key because the speaker is creating a traumatic metaphor of his death through the taking of children away from families by the government, which had occurred in the past. This image is also used to remind the reader of the various traumatic experiences that have and do occur to Native Americans. The stanza ends with despondency on behalf of the speak, and the community as a whole, as the speaker states, "No one really cares or understands / or even wants to" (lines 15–16). These lines reinforce the sense of helplessness that comes with years of horrid actions and trauma. The fact that children were taken from their parents for schooling, for the eradication of language and culture, is well established.

The fourth stanza insinuates that Ace was taken to one of the government schools, where he learned not only how to read and write, but he also learned to drink, do drugs, and have sex, which are stated to be "usual things" for young people:

> He learned to read and to think
> and to drink and to smoke dope
> and to make love,
> just all the usual things, (lines 17–20)

This is in great contrast to what was taught originally in these schools, but the result is the same: the harming and potential destruction of culture. However, the speaker says that Ace was different because of his talent, "except / that he had talent. Wow! / Imagine that! Talent!" (lines 21–23). The exclamations here are out of place with the lines before and after. They are presented in a manner that insinuate sarcasm. The sarcasm is not aimed at the idea that Ace had talent but is suggesting that many would be surprised that Native Americans have what might be considered talent. The speaker reinforces this idea again, later on. Sadly, it is because of this talent that he was killed in a bar:

> So talented was he that
> he was beaten to death
> in a Chicago bar
>   Wow! Talent! (lines 24–27)

Again, the speaker's sarcasm is palpable in the last line of this stanza. The speaker is insinuating that the idea that Native Americans possessing talent is so unacceptable to some that it could lead to death. The talent Ace has is his ability as a painter, and it is with these paintings that the speaker's traumatic figurative language begins to take shape. Furthermore, the physical death could also be symbolic for the cultural death, which could occur if a young person was to express a talent that was considered valuable to white society. In an instance such as that, the person could be pulled away from their home and made to live an existence away from their family, home, and culture.

As the speaker begins to discuss and negotiate with the memory of Ace, it is presented as a struggle, "So what is it I want to say / or want to remember" (lines 28–29). The speaker questions if he should remember the parties ". . . when / we had to help him home," (lines 30–31) or when Ace was ". . . so depressed / at being turned down by a girl?" (lines 32–33). Both of these instances suggest that Ace was depressed and potentially struggling with alcoholism. Although the speaker identifies the alcoholism related to parties and depression associated with being turned down, these problems most likely both stem from another underlying condition within Ace's life.

The seventh stanza discusses a variety of emotions but begins with ambiguity stating, "No, none of these, but all of them," (line 34). The speaker then identifies "all the rage, frustration and confusion, / all the love, tenderness and desperation, / all these things which we carry" (lines 35–37). By presenting these various emotions, the speaker is able to present some of the most powerful emotions that people experience, but the speaker is quick to separate Ace from us by stating:

> . . . but in him
> surged with such energy
> from brain to fingers to pigment
> to living canvas, (lines 38–41)

Ace was able to translate the emotions to artwork, which isn't unusual for artists, but it reinforces the idea that Ace was able to represent something that is unrepresentable and is able to do so without language. The impact on the speaker is made even more significant as he is trying to negotiate the pain of losing a friend and is struggling to do so. But as he looks at Ace's artwork in this moment, he states:

> in those moments I was held,
> like a child witnessing first view
> of the stars, the frightening,
>   wonderous universe. (lines 43–46)

It is as if the speaker is able to truly appreciate Ace's artwork for the first time as he is struggling with emotions born out of Ace's death, for now he is experiencing similar feelings that Ace felt as he created the artwork.

The speaker is able to feel Ace's emotion as he looks at Ace's painting, as is evident in the first lines of the eighth stanza, "His energy was overpowering as he / sketched or painted," (lines 47–48). The stanza continues with the speaker imagining Ace working on his artwork. In order to understand and cope with the death of the speaker's friend, he utilizes traumatic figurative language, which calls upon the history of Native Americans. Ace is a painter, and as the speaker begins discussing one of Ace's paintings, it is through the painting that the speaker implements traumatic figurative language. The act of painting, for Ace, was also a creative outlet for his emotions, as stated in lines 35 through 46. Ace was able to use his painting to overcome both positive and negative emotions, but the subject matter is able to influence the speaker and help him cope with the loss of Ace. The speaker discusses how, in the painting, there are "buffalo and ghost dancers emerging" (line 51). These are references to spiritual and cultural elements within the Native American culture, and as is seen in the lines that follow, the speaker is made to dance as well (line 61), but because it is said that he is forced (line 61), it is evident that the speaker does not dance often. "And his dancers jumped at me / with loud cries, grabbing me, / forcing me to dance" (lines 59–61).

Dance has played, and continues to play, an integral part in the culture of Native Americans, and returning to it, as the speaker is doing in this poem, he is forced to face his cultural past and the trauma that exists therein. The fact that Ace was painting about dance is similar to what is occurring as Native American poets write to promote resistance against the oppressor by using the medium and language of the oppressor. Ace's paintings are a similar resistance against the dominant culture, while within the dominant culture, by using the medium of, mainly, the oppressor. This is, in itself, a type of ambivalence. The idea that dance forces the speaker to reexamine the past becomes clear a few lines later when the poem makes the traumatic figurative language more obvious through the discussion of death and violence. The poem discusses the idea of dancing while a nation was being massacred and while the ghosts of people killed refused to rest:

> I danced
>   as a nation was slaughtered
> and lay broken and bleeding
> I danced
>   among angered ghosts
> who would not lie down gentle
> to death. (lines 70–76)

The speaker was forced to examine the traumatic history of Native Americans in these lines as he recounts the slaughter of his ancestors. The dance here, as was often the case of some Native American dances of the past, is performed in order to celebrate the dead, which is not only the ancestors, but now Ace. The dance of the speaker also becomes an act of resistance where he embodies not only the culture but resistance against death and the racism that cause his friend to die. This resistance occurs in the fact that the speaker moves when his friend cannot and does so to celebrate a culture, which was the reason his friend was murdered. In addition, the angered ghosts (line 74) who were not appeased to remain dead (lines 75–76) are representative of historical trauma that exists within the Native American culture. The angered ghosts *are* traumatic memories. The ghosts are from those who were slaughtered and continue to haunt the speaker as he dances or embraces his cultural heritage.

As the speaker continues, he thinks back to the shortness of Ace's life and expresses "I am bitter now, at this moment" (line 83) and desires to "make him dance / with his dancers, / with me" (lines 85–87). By making Ace one of the dancers, he is forcing him to become part of the cultural trauma of Native Americans and to celebrate the fact that Ace is now part of that ancestry and spiritual legacy. Ace's death is representative of the continuation of historic trauma and existence of trauma, which continues to affect Native Americans presently. At this point the poem reaches its crescendo by drawing the reader in and addressing us directly:

> tears streaming down faces
> limbs jerking in sanity gone fallen,
> and falling into the void of space
> we would clutch and grasp at
> each and every one of you
> and force you into the dance

> and rub your face into the gore
> so proudly you helped create. (lines 88–95)

The speaker presents three very important elements in the stanza that need to be addressed. First, in line 89, the dancers cry with their "limbs jerking with sanity gone fallen," thereby demonstrating the intense emotion they are experiencing through dance. This emotion is complex, and given the other emotions of the poem, one can expect the emotions to be related to mourning and frustration. The speaker's mention of "sanity gone fallen" (line 89) and the dancers "falling into the void of space" (line 90) indicates a feeling of helplessness and isolation. The isolation is not an individual isolation, but the isolation of the group as they are falling in the nothingness. The speaker then turns and pulls the reader directly into the poem and wants to make the reader join in the dance. By doing this, the speaker is attempting to bring the reader in to share the emotions that are being expressed and felt. By doing this, the speaker is attempting to form a community beyond the one that exists. A larger community would be beneficial and could give a greater opportunity of healing.

The speaker also attempts to force those outside of the culture to experience the feelings of this historical and cultural trauma. This idea is conveyed in lines 94 and 95. In these lines, the speaker is forcing the audience to confront the historical trauma. The speaker also passes blame on to the speaker by telling the audience (presumably not Native American) that it created this trauma. The speaker feels the need for someone to blame for the death of Ace, and by using traumatic figurative language of the atrocities committed against Native Americans historically, the speaker is able to attribute the death to the same people who killed Ace's ancestors. By using traumatic figurative language, the speaker finds someone to blame and is also better able to cope with the loss of his friend by attributing his death to the same type of hatred and violence committed against Native Americans in the past.

Just as the speaker begins to place the blame upon others, he reverses his position in the final stanza and expresses the futility of fighting, "And what's the use, and what's the use" (line 96). This floundering feeling of inconsequence immediately shifts in the lines that follow as, "my mind screams to the shadows, / so many of our youth / gone into death," (lines 97–99). Although, given the preceding line, the speaker sees little benefit in placing blame, the fact that it is the speaker's mind screaming indicates that is it not a verbal scream but a traumatic response to Ace's death as well as a history of so many young people who have died.

Whereas the speaker has shifted blame from "you" to no one, the speaker then continues his ambivalence in the next stanza by placing his blame on everyone:

> and all the blame and blood
> and all the justifications
> And explanations,
>   add up
> to a loss we all share the deed of. (lines 100–105)

By doing this, the speaker moves past the idea of pointing blame and encouraging everyone to take responsibility, calling not only for an act of resistance on the part of Native Americans, but for everyone to resist the ignorance of racism and work toward a peaceful community built on equality. Just as he says this, though, he returns back to Native Americans and tells them to confront the historic trauma and to try to work through it rather than run from it and let the traumatic history be forgotten:

> it is us, the runaways,
> the self-made outcasts,
> it is to our grief
> that we are forgetting
>   the dance. (lines 107–111)

Therefore, traumatic figurative language plays two roles in this poem. First, it allows the speaker to cope with the loss of his friend, but it also calls on Native Americans to engage the historic trauma. The speaker is taking an event of racism, and the massive stressors and emotion involved in losing a friend to murder and directs the anguish toward the unresolved historical grief that resides for some within the Native American culture. The death of Ace is a traumatic metaphor for the treatment of Native Americans currently and historically. This is similar to what occurred in the poems by Japanese Americans as discussed in chapter 2. Much like Yamada's discussion in her poem "Cincinnati," an event is used to examine and discuss traumatic events of the past.

LINDA HOGAN: TRAUMATIC FIGURATIVE LANGUAGE AND THE RECLAIMING OF A DIVIDED SELF

Thus far, traumatic figurative language has presented oppression against Native Americans in the form of battles of the past and by comparing the historic trauma to the oppression and pain that the speakers engage with at the present, which has generated the isolation and unhomeliness some Native Americans feel. By using images from the former prison, Alcatraz, Blue Cloud's speakers were able to demonstrate a sense of empowerment by reclaiming culture and suggested that such reclaiming is beneficial to one's sense of self and overall identity. Linda Hogan was selected for this study because of her discussion of internal conflicts occurring within the mind of people born of different ethnicities who once warred with one another. This is another play of ambivalence, which is an overarching theme among the three writers of this study. The speakers' internal conflict, as shall be demonstrated, is also a call to resist the conformity with the oppressive culture and to create a stronger tie to her Native American heritage. Her poetry engages the difficulty a person may have with this cultural heritage, and the speakers in the poems are able to articulate the stress and emotion tied to historic trauma by means of traumatic figurative language.

Unlike the other Native American poets examined, a good deal has been written about Linda Hogan's poetry over the last ten years. Janet McAdams examines Hogan's collection *Rounding the Human Corners* in her essay "'Ways in the World': Formal Poetics in Linda Hogan's *Rounding the Human Corners*."[29] McAdams does briefly discuss the themes of violence, hegemony, and the idea of healing in the poems of this collection, but nothing is mentioned about trauma. An article that does examine trauma within Hogan's writing is Catherine Kunce's "Feasting on Famine in Linda Hogan's *Solar Storms*,"[30] but the literature that Kunce is examining is a novel rather than poetry. Nevertheless, Kunce's examination is significant in its focus on how Hogan calls on the reader to "listen" throughout the novel and the discussion that Kunce places on historical trauma, although not specifically articulated as such. Kunce is not alone in the examination of *Solar Storms* for trauma, as Irene Vernon also examines the idea of trauma within her article "'We Were Those Who Walked out of Bullets and Hunger': Representations of Trauma and Healing in *Solar Storms*."[31] Vernon's article gives a more in-depth analysis of the historical trauma being voiced within the novel, but Vernon, unlike Kunce, discusses the idea of reconstructing identity and reestablishing a sense of being, which can be done through storytelling. Although the examinations are welcome, both analyses focus on prose rather than poetry. Other articles have been written about trauma within Hogan's *Solar Storms*, like Summer Harrison's "'We Need New Stories': Trauma, Storytelling, and Mapping of Environmental Injustice in Linda Hogan's *Solar Storms* and Standing Rock,"[32] yet articles examining Hogan's poetry through a trauma lens are virtually nonexistent from the past ten years.

In Hogan's poem "The Truth Is,"[33] the speaker expresses her difficulty with identity as a war and strong distrust between the white and Native

American heritage that resides inside her. The speaker identifies herself as partially Chickasaw and partially white in the first stanza as she discusses her hands in her pockets, which she identifies as different races:

> In my left pocket a Chickasaw hand
> rests on the bone of the pelvis.
> In my right pocket
> a white hand. Don't worry. It's mine. (lines 1–4)

Although these lines appear to do little more than identify the ethnic heritage of the speaker, it is the second half of line 4 and line 5 that suggests the poem explores ideas surrounding the distrust of whites, as she reassures the reader that the white hand belongs to her and not someone trying to steal from her, ". . . Don't worry. It's mine / and not some thief's" (lines 4–5). This distrust is exacerbated by the left hand (Chickasaw) resting against her pelvis, which is quite intimate, yet the right hand is only passingly described, and yet it is the one the reader is reassured about by the speaker. These lines set up the speaker's traumatic figurative language within the poem for a conflict to arise between the two identities. To recall DuBois's idea of double conscious, it is evident that this theory is at play in Hogan's poem. However, the speaker has a divided and ambivalent identity, not as much in her public self, but internally.

In the second stanza, the speaker continues to discuss the idea of belonging to two different races and mentions how she would desire harmony between the two, but such harmony seems impossible. In the first half of the stanza, she presents this hope for harmony by saying of her hands, "I am a tree, grafted branches / bearing two kinds of fruit, / apricots maybe and pit cherries" (lines 12–15). The harmony between the races within the speaker is short lived. As the stanza continues, the speaker reveals that the two ethnicities are at conflict within her and she longs for amnesty:

> It's not that way. The truth is
> We are crowded together
> and knock against each other at night.
> We want amnesty. (lines 17–19)

Clearly, the speaker is conflicted about her identity and the idea of harboring the history of two groups who warred against one another within herself. This is, as one might imagine, a result, at least partially, of historic trauma, which the speaker must confront when attempting to come to grips with her identity. The trauma is at least partially evident as she demonstrates the distrust for whites, even within her own identity.

The third stanza begins with the speaker addressing herself. This is only evident because the speaker addresses herself again in the fifth stanza. Because the speaker has already identified herself as having a divided existence by being partially white and partially Chickasaw, it is not surprising to find her talking to herself, "Linda, girl, I keep telling you" (line 20) and suggesting that it does not really matter who loved and who killed who, "this is nonsense / about who loved who / and who killed who" (lines 21–23). By doing so, the speaker is trying to move beyond the traumatic history of clashes that existed between the two cultures that once fought and, in her familial history, loved one another. By speaking about the traumatic history, she is trying to minimize the specter of her history and the feelings she continues to encounter based on this history. She is, in essence, telling the trauma in order to find a type of resolution and peace. Furthermore, she is presenting herself in the first and third persons, which reinforces the idea of loss of identity. As such, the speaker produces an ambivalent sense of self who wishes to negotiate the complexities of a bifurcated identity divided between histories of oppressor and oppressed, while also having to face the legacy of trauma. This legacy is one in which her ancestors were both oppressor and oppressed, killer and killed, and she is forced to confront a history that is at constant odds yet try to find singularity of self within this division. As such, even her sense of self is ambivalent and relegated to an objectified third person.

In the fourth stanza, the speaker refers to the ". . . Civilian Conservation Corps" (line 25), which is significant due to its importance in United States and Native American history. The Civilian Conservation Corps (CCC) was developed during the Franklin Roosevelt administration to help families earn additional (or an) income. A specialized division was created for Native Americans. This program was significant because Native Americans were eventually given the same rate of pay as their white counterparts[34] and they were given additional freedoms their white counterparts did not share. While whites were forced to live in the camps, Native Americans were given the freedom to return home from the camp,[35] and special projects were set aside strictly to improve the reservations where many Native Americans lived.[36] Although the inclusion of this program in the poem could be to illustrate an historic equality between Native Americans and whites, the speaker's mention of the CCC is due to the negative impact felt by Native Americans when the program ended. Calvin W. Gower notes in his article, "The CCC Indian Division," that "the demise of the CCC was a severe setback to the American Indian."[37] The reason for this setback resided in the economic position most Native Americans faced at that time. "CCC payments, although small, did give poverty-stricken Indian employees and their families a financial boost when they probably needed it most."[38] What is perhaps equally important is the way the "CCC did not force the Indians to adjust to the white man's way of living but instead—following the recommendations of Indian Service leaders—deliberately altered the organization, and program to harmonize with the ways of the reservation life."[39] In addition, it cannot be overlooked that although whites and Native Americans were eventually paid equally, they were still segregated. This was also the idea that many in the American Indian Movement, occurring many years later, wanted to embrace: equality in representation and treatment with a culture separate from the white oppressor.

Returning to the poem, the speaker describes herself as having empty pockets (line 27) and referring to the "Civilian Conservation Corps" (line 25). The empty pockets harken to the setback for post-CCC Native Americans but is also significant in regard to the mention of pockets in the beginning of the poem that aid in the speaker's identification of herself. To reference the CCC in a metaphorical fashion calls attention to the extreme poverty felt by Native Americans at that time and compare it to the difficulty of working through the adversarial identities as outlined by the speaker. The remainder of the stanza focuses on these empty pockets and says of them, "It's just as well since they are masks / for the soul . . ." (lines 27–28). Therefore, the speaker is referencing the idea for which the previous metaphor was being used to discuss identity because the masks used for the soul could be the identity and physical traits of the human body. The poem takes a turn as it references the idea of property having teeth, ". . . since coins and keys / both have the sharp teeth of property" (lines 29–30). The implication here is that property, identified as coins and keys, is dangerous and could harm the possessor because the question for property was key in the advancement of imperialism, capitalism, and the Native American oppression. Given the context of the previous lines of the stanza, one could read the lines as saying that in the past, wealth, or lack thereof, has had a traumatizing effect on Native Americans. If one takes into consideration how nearly everything was taken from Native Americans historically, including the very land they lived on and their culture, the idea of property being dangerous resides in the idea that it can be taken away. This is evident in this stanza alone as the speaker discusses the CCC and the idea of the Great Depression, which affected people worldwide. The historical impact of loss within the speaker stems from historical trauma and loss, thus creating anxiety about the idea of having possessions to begin with. To have possessions, therefore, is to be vulnerable to having them taken away, creating further anxiety and distress.

The fifth stanza begins in much the same way the third stanza begins, with the speaker addressing herself, but instead of addressing herself as "Linda," as she did in line 20, she addresses herself as "girl" (line 31). She continues by discussing how "it is dangerous to be a woman of two countries" (line 32). These lines allow the speaker to present herself as having a divided identity. By doing so, she is then able to continue the traumatic figurative language in the lines that follow. In lines 34 through 37, the speaker calls upon the violent past of whites and Native Americans in these lines by writing about fear, calling one pocket the enemy, and about the idea of knowing how to fight:

> . . . Even though
> you walk and whistle like you aren't afraid
> you know which pocket the enemy lives in
> and you remember how to fight
> so you better keep right on walking. (lines 34–38)

These themes of fear and fighting are developed by the lines previous where she discusses her pockets and her divided identity. As the poem continues, the traumatic history becomes blatantly articulated in line 39 where she states, "And you remember who killed who" which directly contradicts the ideas in the third stanza when the speaker stated that it was nonsense to think about who killed whom (lines 20–23). This reinforces the idea of ambivalence that resonates within the poem.

The stanza concludes with what could be identified as reoccurring nightmares, which often plague survivors of trauma events. The final two lines of this stanza read, "and there's that knocking on the door / in the middle of the night" (lines 41–42). The implicature of the language suggests the knocking is a reoccurring event. The speaker does not identify the knocking as a singular event, but she refers to it with the word "that," a demonstrative adjective, which indicates repeated action. Because it happens in the "middle of the night" (line 42), because of the focus on hands as representative of identity and in connection with historic trauma, and because knocking is generated by hands, logic dictates that the knocking is a metaphor for reoccurring nightmares. The existence of these nightmares in the speaker reinforces the traumatic figurative language by suggesting that the existence of trauma manifesting itself in the nightmares is an allied and ancillary symptom of trauma.

As the poem concludes, the speaker tells herself to focus on other things in order to not think about the trauma that has manifested in her nightmares:

> Relax, there are other things to think about.
> Shoes for instance.
> Now those are the true masks of the soul
> The left shoe
> and the right one with its white foot. (lines 43–47)

She moves her thoughts to her shoes and begins the same thought process that she had about her hands and pockets. The speaker has brought us full circle in an attempt to demonstrate how, regardless of what is being thought of, the traces of historical trauma infect every aspect of the speaker's life. She is unable to find peace because she is at war internally with her divided identity and the historical trauma that is associated with her Chickasaw self. The traumatic figurative language used to discuss this struggle helps the speaker show her audience how painful and troubling these aspects of her life are, and she is able to bring the historic past to the reader's mind, so one is forced to remember the past and see how it continues to affect people presently.

As demonstrated, Hogan's speakers use traumatic figurative language and call on historic elements of our past in order to discuss the difficulties many people with a multicultural heritage may face. By using traumatic figurative language, Hogan's speaker allows the reader to gain insight into how heritages such as this can create difficulties for an individual attempting to formulate his/her own identity. Like much of the poetry of this chapter, the speaker in Hogan's poem plays a great deal with ambivalence. It is evident that the speaker desires to make peace with the idea of having two cultural backgrounds. She discusses this desire in several locations within the poem but continues returning to the inability to find the peace she yearns to have within herself. This is also indicative of a suppressed desire for resistance. After the speaker states she needs to think of more important things, the schism appears again at the end of the poem when the speaker begins to talk of her feet. This demonstrates that the speaker is resisting the urge to resist; she refuses to answer her own call to supplant her white ancestral heritage and reclaim her Native American heritage. In the section that follows, the speaker in Hogan's poem continues to examine identity and the difficulties that many face by using abjection and unhomeliness within the poem. Like Blue Cloud, some speakers in Hogan's poems demonstrate abjection and unhomeliness through the use of travel and displacement while also demonstrating how some choose to maintain their original cultural identities as they are being displaced while others attempt to discard their historic past.

ABJECTION AND THE QUEST FOR CULTURAL IDENTITY IN THE POETRY OF LINDA HOGAN

As has been demonstrated, Hogan's speakers are able to use traumatic figurative language to represent historical trauma in her poetry. Although the utilization of traumatic figurative language is beneficial for presenting trauma,

Hogan speakers, like the speakers of many other poets, are able to present trauma by other means. The final poem examined in this chapter, "Cities behind Glass,"[40] focuses on abjection and unhomeliness through the eyes of a woman wandering in a place that remains unidentified. Nearly everything about the woman remains unsaid as she looks at the world around her, which seems foreign and is filled with immigrants. As such, not only does the poem discuss the speaker seeing people who appear displaced, but the speaker feels displaced as well. In addition, both she and the place remain without identity, which follows the idea of abjection closely. What is most pronounced in the poem is the quest to reclaim and reestablish a cultural identity. Windows and glass play a key role as shall be seen through the examination of the poem and the quest to establish a cultural identity.

Travel is presented early in the poem as it identifies a family traveling, but the speaker recognizes them as both traveling together and as traveling alone, "Dusty light falls through windows / where entire families journey together, alone" (lines 1–2). Therefore, the idea of ambivalence is also immediately apparent as the family appears to be both together and alone. Although it is not clear whether these families are traveling for recreation or because of being dislocated, what is shown, very early on, is the idea of travel. This ambivalence is significant because, as the poem is a discussion of reclaiming or keeping one's heritage, the ambivalence of the families here demonstrates that this is a cross-cultural problem. The ambiguity in travel is also significant because in these first lines the reader is looking at the families from behind glass. They are witnessed traveling, although the reader is not told why, thus their ambiguity also resides in their uncertainty of heritage, which will become evident later. As the poem continues, it shows "Mothers open the sills and shake the old world / from lace tablecloths" (lines 3–4). People are attempting to lose their original cultural identity by trying to "shake the old world / from their tablecloths" (lines 3–4) with "old world" being a very loaded phrase associated with culture and heritage. The mothers try to discard this identity from an item, which is associated with a strong cultural element: food. This woman, like the people traveling in the streets, does not have this protective glass in front of her, which is metaphoric for the embracing of one's cultural identity.

As the poem continues, it shows immigrant women riding on buses, "Beneath flowered babushkas / immigrant women put their faith in city buses" (lines 5–6). The speaker identifies the women wearing babushkas, a scarf worn primarily by older Russian women, as being immigrants, yet, unlike the women in the first stanza, these women still cling to their cultural heritage as evident by the resting of their heads, and babushka, against the glass. In addition, babushka is not only head garment, but it is also an endearing term used for an old woman or grandmother. These women, who are also traveling, are also seen behind glass:

> They take refuge behind glass,
> lay their heads against windows.
> Behind veined eyelids
> they journey. (lines 7–10)

Unlike the women of the previous stanza who discarded cultural connections by shaking the old world (line 3) from their tablecloths out of an open window, these women sit behind closed windows. Their heads, covered by babushkas, lie against the windows. In opposing stanzas, customs are first being interrupted (the tablecloths are having their cultural character effaced by being shaken in a window), and subsequently, the custom of the babushka is maintained (by resting the cultural signifier against a closed window). These women, unlike the women of the first stanza, are traveling rather than residing in a home and are visibly tired. The women appear displaced because of how they maintain their cultural heritage and because of the travel that they are making. This suggests, in part, that maintaining one's cultural heritage and resisting an oppressive culture has the potential to be a struggle and tiring, especially when one would be considered an outsider and displaced. The images show elements of displacement and the difficulty some people face when they cling to their cultural heritage, which may be partially due to historical trauma as well as resistance against the oppressive culture. The actions of the women on the bus, and the fact their eyelids are veined (line 9), demonstrate the distress they are encountering, especially given their age, regardless of where it stems. One cannot discount the fact these women are journeying as the speaker makes clear at the end of the stanza.

What is not clear is their destination. The first line of the third stanza identifies their possible destination: "Brussels, perhaps, is their destination / where older women make lace," (lines 11–12). Brussels is renowned for lace made by the old women who live there; therefore, it is an embedded custom for Belgians. Ironically, the Russian women may be put in a situation where their customs are yielded to that of others; the Russians, those of the East who are the other, will have their cultural customs assimilated into another set of Western customs with them being immigrants in a subaltern position, retaining the nineteenth-century paradigm of the superiority of Western European culture. The women on the bus not only are old but are going to work. The need to work at an older age, as the speaker imagines these women to be doing, would reflect further stressors in their lives, especially stress that refers to loss of resources. In addition, it is important to note that these women cling to their cultural identity even though they work in a different culture and manufacture culturally crafted goods. Not only do these older women have to work, but they may not be well paid for their labors. As a result, the stress is intensified.

The fourth stanza returns back to glass, which is the most significant symbol of the poem, "On the street / invisible panes of glass are strapped / to the sides of a truck" (lines 15–17). The glass, as described as being strapped (line 16), reinforces the idea of poverty. Glass, thus far, has been the symbolic locus of identity for the first two groups of women. The first had tossed her cultural heritage out the glassless window, and the second rests part of her cultural identity against the glass of a moving bus. This stanza reinforces the idea by saying (of the glass strapped to the truck) that it shows the world with people traveling, but, most importantly, it shows horses that are purposefully described as red, "The world shows through \ filled with people, with red horses" (lines 18–19). The glass acts as a mirror in this stanza and focuses on a horse. The horses are said to be wearing blinders, and, although they are described as slow, they are said to be running inside, "Inside that slow horse flesh / behind blinders / the dark animals are running," (lines 21–23). Because the speaker identifies the animals running inside, and yet they are described as having blinders over their eyes, these images are occurring within the horse's mind, or rather, the speaker's imagination of the operations of the horse's mind. The slow-moving horse desires to be elsewhere, and given that these horses (line 19) are described as dark (line 23), the speaker is suggesting the horse is depressed or maintains a negative mind-set. The imagined mental escape for the horse resides in the desire to run, which is the opposite of its present situation. As the speaker continues, she discusses the horses as being both shadow and light, which presents more ambivalence in the poem, as the horses are seen running in America, "shadow horses, / horse of light / running across American hills" (lines 24–26). Thus, the speaker is showing the horse, as it is reflected through pane of glass, thinking about her own desire to be running through America. The horse is also dislocated as it desires to be back in America running through the hills where it once called home. The speaker sees the horse as maintaining its identity because it is reflected in the glass.

The horse, like the woman on the bus, is traveling for work, but their double identities are reflected in both in the glass and in their descriptions. Although this travel does pertain to their locus of identity, given the horse's imagined thought of untamed American landscapes and the Russian woman's babushka, these lines suggest more of a focus on unhomeliness through a forced or necessary removal rather than abjection. If one assumes the horse to be in the streets of Europe at work, the horse might represent another double or triple layer of displacement as the wild American horses were descended from Spanish conquistadors' horses brought from Europe. The horses ultimately came from Arabia during the Islamic jihad, which began in the century after the Prophet Mohammed's death. Thus, there is a kind of double/triple displacement across generations with the horses compared to the multiple moves Native Americans were forced to make as treaty after treaty was broken and Nations were pushed and displaced repeatedly. The horse, or workhorse, is displaced at the whim and in need of the stronger force, man, just as the Native American is displaced and unhomed by the oppressor, the European.

Strong indications of abjection do not materialize until the last stanza. The speaker appears to be coping with unhomeliness, and she is also describing elements of abjection. The speaker of the poem is experiencing a distorted world where everything is, as she says, "Everything is foreign here" (line 27), and as she experiences this unhomeliness, she is walking the streets of the city observing what she deems as foreign, which is very representative of Fuchs' definition. "No on sees me. / No one see this woman walking city streets" (28–29). The world the speaker has described is also very fragmented and jumps from image to image, giving only brief examinations of each. One cannot be sure where the women on the bus are going, and the speaker does not give the location of where the poem is taking place. What is given is movement, from families who are journeying in the first stanza to the grandmothers in the second and third stanzas to the horse in the fourth and finally to the speaker herself. All are traveling, and none appears to have a place to call home. The most telling line of the poem, which demonstrates that trauma is occurring, is when the speaker says, "No one sees the animals running inside my skin," (line 30). The speaker is using this metaphor to identify the feeling of flight, which the speaker feels as she travels through a land where everything seems foreign. The speaker finishes the poem with threatening images, such as the word dark in line 32. The darkness presented in the forest of line 31 makes the previous images more troubling and reinforces the feelings of trauma. She states in the final lines that the grandmothers, who like the horses are described as dark (line 32), are looking out of her eyes, much like the women of the bus, and are watching all that is going on as they travel, "the deep forest of southern trees, / the dark grandmothers looking out through my eyes, / taking it in, traveling still" (lines 30–33). By presenting the feelings in this manner, the speaker is able to use the previous images of the horse and women alongside her travels and her feelings of isolation, presented as no one seeing her, to produce a representation of trauma. The final two lines give the impression that the speaker has been traveling for a long time and does not appear to be stopping soon. Thus, the trauma the speaker is presenting is unresolved, and it is through this constant movement that she is able to cope. The displaced old women in babushkas and the horses stand in as metaphorical representations of the speaker's plight, but they are also to exist behind the protective glass of cultural heritage.

Images, like those of travel, are brought to the reader's attention by their placement within the poem. These images force the reader to focus on that particular image or idea because it comprises an entire line. This is unique to poetry because the poet has the ability to draw a reader's attention to images or ideas in this manner. Poets also have the ability to focus a reader's attention on certain words by their placement within the poem. In this poem, words such as windows (lines 1 and 8) and glass (line 7) are placed at the end of the line to draw the reader's attention and reinforce the image of windows. More significant, however, are words like "alone" (line 2), "journey" (line 10), "destination" (line 11), "street" (line 15), "streets" (lines 20 and 29), "running" (line 23), and "traveling" (line 33) to reinforce the idea of travel within the poem. The reader is forced to pay special attention to these words, and one confronts the idea of travel within the poem because of the placement of these words. Many of the words are not only indicative of travel, but they are suggesting unhomeliness, which was echoed many times through the stanzas of the poem. Many in the poem are struggling with identity, like the women shaking the old world out of tablecloths, and many are dislocated from their homes.

The speaker is moving outside of the glass and says that no one sees her and how things are foreign to her. Beneath her skin, like beneath the horse's blinders, there are animals running, and given the horse is said to be displaced from America, she may be as well. Her grandmothers who are able to see through her eyes (line 32) demonstrate a desire to reconnect with her cultural heritage. These ancestors are alive within her; thus, she still has ties, yet she is able to find home within the world as she travels. This ambivalence is significant as the speaker knows of her ancestors, and, for her, they still reside inside her, yet she is also unable to find home within her heritage in that she is both unhomed and unable to cling to or throw away a heritage as the other women in the poem do through the imagery that is presented. She is unseen, while the women discarding their heritage are witnessed, and symbols of their heritage are seen to be discarded while others are clung to in the form of their babushkas. What is seen, like in Hogan's other poem, is an ambivalent attempt to resist cultural oppression and establish cultural ties to one's heritage, but restrained in "The Truth Is" and the inability to do so as evident with the invisibility of the speaker in this poem.

As discussed, the poem uses its form, particularly lines and line breaks, to focus the reader's attention on specific images and ideas to bring forth the idea and experience of trauma. In addition, Hogan's speakers use abjection and unhomeliness to show influence of massive stressors and trauma that individuals within the narrative of the poem may feel as they cope with displacement. These, as well as the use of traumatic figurative language, are common in poetry confronting and discussing trauma. The use of these techniques, although not unique to Hogan's poetry, are utilized very effectively and allow the reader to gain a greater insight into feelings of those who are enduring the effect of massive stressors and trauma. The speakers in Hogan's poems, like others throughout this chapter, play with ambivalence. While the speakers in Blue Cloud and Coffee's poems push toward resistance of the oppressor, it is precisely in this resistance that one can find the ambivalence in Hogan's poems. In "The Truth Is," the speaker wishes to make peace with the two cultural heritages that reside within her, but there is ambivalence in that, although she states she wants peace, she is unable to see beyond the struggle. As has been stated, she resists the resistance consciously, but appears to want to resist subconsciously. In "Cities behind Glass," the speaker's ambivalence resides in her need to find her cultural heritage, which is evident in her traveling, yet her heritage is abundantly apparent as she discusses how her grandmothers look out her eyes. The searching that the speaker needs to undertake is internal rather than external.

NOTES

1. "Indian Health Disparities," *Indian Health Service*, United States Department of Health and Human Services. Accessed October 19, 2018.

2. Maria Yellow Horse Brave Heart, "The Historical Trauma Response among Natives and Its Relationship to Substance Abuse: A Lakota Illustration," in *Healing and Mental Health for Native Americans: Speaking in Red*, ed. Ethan Nebelkopf and Mary Phillips (Lanham, MD: Altamira, 2004), 7.

3. Heart, "Historical Trauma Response," 7.

4. Heart, "Historical Trauma Response," 9.

5. Robin Coffee, "Voices in the Water," in *A Scar upon Our Voice* (Albuquerque: University of New Mexico Press, 2005), 7.

6. Robin Coffee, *A Scar upon Our Voice* (Albuquerque: University of New Mexico Press, 2005).

7. Robin Coffee, "In from the Cold," in *A Scar upon Our Voice* (Albuquerque: University of New Mexico Press, 2005), 14.

8. Robin Coffee, "No Other Way," in *A Scar upon Our Voice* (Albuquerque: University of New Mexico Press, 2005), 22.

9. Robin Coffee, "Warriors of This Time," in *A Scar upon Our Voice* (Albuquerque: University of New Mexico Press, 2005), 70.

10. Robin Coffee, "Blood of a Warrior," in *A Scar upon Our Voice* (Albuquerque: University of New Mexico Press, 2005), 76.

11. Howard Zinn, *A People's History of the United States* (New York: Harper Collins, 2005), 25.

12. Peter Blue Cloud, "Alcatraz," in *Clans of Many Nations* (Fredonia, NY: White Pine, 1995), 39.

13. "Civil War at Alcatraz." *National Park Service*. United States Department of the Interior. Accessed October 28, 2018.

14. Troy Johnson, "We Hold the Rock: The Alcatraz Indian Occupation." United States Department of the Interior. *National Park Service.* Accessed October 28, 2018.

15. Johnson, "We Hold the Rock."

16. Troy Johnson, "The Occupation of Alcatraz Island: Roots of American Indian Activism," *Wicazo Sa Review* 10, no. 2 (1994): 76.

17. Ibid.

18. Ibid.

19. Ibid., 64.

20. Ibid.

21. Lee Irwin, "Freedom, Law, and Prophecy: A Brief History of Native American Religious Resistance," in *American Indians and U.S. Politics*, edited by John M. Meyer (Westport, CT: Praeger Publishers, 2002), 83.

22. Irwin, "Freedom, Law, and Prophecy."

23. Stephan Cornell, "The New Indian Politics," in *American Indians and U.S. Politics*, edited by John M. Meyer (Westport, CT: Praeger Publishers, 2002), 103.

24. Johnson, "The Occupation of Alcatraz Island," 77.

25. "kachina," in *Chambers Dictionary of the Unexplained*, edited by Una McGovern (Chambers Harrap, 2007).

26. "kachina," in *Britannica Concise Encyclopedia*, by Encyclopaedia Britannica (Britannica Digital Learning, 2017).

27. "Coyote Hills Regional Park," *East Bay Regional Park District*. Accessed September 3, 2019.

28. Peter Blue Cloud, "For Ace," in *Clans of Many Nations* (Fredonia, NY: White Pine, 1995), 100–103.

29. Janet McAdams, "'Ways in the World': Formal Poetics in Linda Hogan's *Rounding the Human Corners*," *The Kenyon Review* 32, no. 1 (2010): 226–35.

30. Catherine Kunce, "Feasting on Famine in Linda Hogan's *Solar Storms*." *Studies in American Indian Literatures* 21, no. 2 (2009): 50–70.

31. Irene S. Vernon, "'We Were Those Who Walked out of Bullets and Hunger': Representation of Trauma and Healing in *Solar Storms*," *American Indian Quarterly* 36, no. 1 (2012): 34–49.

32. Summer Harrison, "'We Need New Stories': Trauma, Storytelling, and the Mapping of Environmental Injustice in Linda Hogan's *Solar Storms* and Standing Rock," *American Indian Quarterly* 43, no. 1 (2019): 1–35.

33. Linda Hogan, "The Truth Is," in *Seeing through the Sun* (Amherst: University of Massachusetts Press, 1985), 4–5.

34. Calvin W. Gower, "The CCC Indian Division: Aid for Depressed Americans, 1933–1942," *Minnesota History* 43, no. 1 (1972): 10.

35. Ibid., 6.

36. Ibid., 11–12.
37. Ibid., 13.
38. Ibid.
39. Ibid.
40. Linda Hogan, "Cities behind Glass," in *Seeing through the Sun* (Amherst: University of Massachusetts Press, 1985), 59.

Afterword

As the language may indicate, literary trauma theory borrows a great deal from postcolonial theory and has the ability to further the ideas of postcolonial thought by contributing to psychological aspects of the theory. Literary trauma theory is not reliant on postcolonial thought or subject matter as future endeavors of the theory can be applied not only to other poets of these respective groups, but also to other groups that have incurred trauma and continue to incur trauma to this day. It should be evident that while this study did examine African American, Japanese American, and Native American poetry, there are numerous poets from each culture whose work would readily lend itself to a literary trauma lens. One example well worth studying is the poetry of Yusef Komunyakaa as a poet who engages historical trauma within African American culture as well as direct trauma incurred during his time spent in the Vietnam War. Many speakers within Komunyakaa's poems discuss, not only the conflict and struggle with racism and African American historical trauma, but several poems, especially in his collection *Dien Cai Dau*, discuss what it means to be a black soldier in combat during segregation that was carried over with the soldiers to Vietnam.

Further studies utilizing literary trauma theory would be quite beneficial for study in many different fields of literature from various communities. Poetry from the gay and lesbian community, like that of Frank O'Hara, Rafael Campo, and Adrienne Rich, would lend itself to the examination of literary trauma theory. Given the continued struggle for equality that the gay and lesbian community continue to endure, and the vile hatred that permeates the media and our culture, poetry dealing with massive stressors and trauma from direct exposure to violence and hatred will unfortunately continue for some time. Additionally, poetry from the Chicano/a and Latino/a communities, like that of Martin Espada, Gary Soto, Sonia Sanchez, Jimmy Santiago

Baca, and Lorna Dee Cervantes, would benefit greatly from the application of literary trauma theory. Given the long history of racism against Chicano/a and Latino/a Americans, not only would the poetry from this community benefit from examination of the poetry as it relates to historic trauma, but the current anti-Mexican (and ultimately anti-Latino/a) climate that pervades the media and society is continuing the perpetuation of massive stressors and trauma associated with racism and hate.

Finally, a third community of poets that benefit from exploration using literary trauma theory is that of Arabic American writers. Poets such as Naomi Shihab Nye and other contemporary Arab American writers would be of great interest because of the post-9/11 racism against Muslims and Arab Americans. By no means does this discount the fact that anti-Arabic sentiments have permeated our culture for hundreds of years, but the influx of hatred driven by the response to 9/11 has greatly impacted the Arabic American community, and the writings that emanate from that community are and will be filled with both direct and historical trauma. Writings from nearly every culture and genre have the potential to be enriched by examination from literary trauma theory. As more texts are examined using the theory, more research needs to be conducted within the theory itself to keep literary trauma theory abreast with contemporary thoughts of psychological ideas of trauma.

What may be most apparent in our current political climate is that trauma is affecting many people and many cultures. From the horrific shootings that have become all too commonplace to the rhetoric that both manufactures racism and waves the flames of old hate, there undoubtedly will be new literature written as people try to tell their stories by means of prose, poetry, drama, and song. As we learn to listen and attempt to understand feelings, ideas, and pains that may be beyond the scope of our understanding and representation, we may find that not only does telling trauma help survivors cope but reading about the traumas may help survivors understand that they are not alone.

Bibliography

Auerhahn, Nanette, and Dori Laub. "Intergenerational Memory of the Holocaust." In *International Handbook of Multigenerational Legacies of Trauma*, edited by Yael Danieli, 21–41. New York: Plenum, 1998.
Baraka, Amiri. "Black Dada Nihilismus." In *The LeRoi Jones/Amiri Baraka Reader*, edited by William J. Harris, 71–73. New York: Thundermouth, 1991.
Baraka, Amiri. "Legacy." Poetry Foundation. Accessed October 25, 2018,
Baraka, Amiri. "Reggae or Not." In *Transbluesency: Selected Poems*, 175–85. New York: Marsilio, 1995.
Baraka, Imamu Amiri. *The Music: Reflections on Jazz and Blues.* New York: William Morrow and Company, 1987.
Bleger, Jose. *Symbiosis and Ambiguity*. Edited by John Churcher and Leopoldo Bleger. Translated by Susan Rogers, Leopoldo Bleger, and John Churcher. New York: Routledge, 2013.
Blue Cloud, Peter. "Alcatraz." In *Clans of Many Nations*, 39. Fredonia, NY: White Pine, 1995.
Blue Cloud, Peter. "For Ace." In *Clans of Many Nations*, 100–103. Fredonia, NY: White Pine, 1995.
Brassaw, Mandolin. "The Light That Came to Lucille Clifton: Beyond Lucille and Lucifer." *MELUS* 37, no. 3 (2012): 43–70.
Brave Heart, Maria Yellow Horse. "The Historical Trauma Response among Natives and Its Relationship to Substance Abuse: A Lakota Illustration." In *Healing and Mental Health for Native Americans: Speaking in Red*, edited by Ethan Nebelkopf and Mary Phillips. Lanham, MD: Altamira, 2004.
Brooks, Cleanth. *The Well Wrought Urn.* Orlando: Harcourt, 1975.
Brown, Melissa J., and Marcus W. Feldman. "Sociocultural Epistasis and Cultural Exaptation in Footbinding, Marriage Form, and Religious Practices in the Early 20th-Century Taiwan." *PNAS*. December 29, 2009. Accessed June 13, 2019.
Burt, Ryan. "Interning America's Colonial History: The Anthologies and Poetry of Lawson Fusao Inada." *MELUS* 35, no. 3 (2010): 105–30.

"Civil War at Alcatraz." *National Park Service.* United States Department of the Interior. Accessed October 28, 2018.

Clifton, Lucille. "if something should happen." In *Good Times*, 21. New York: Random House, 1969.

Clifton, Lucille. "in the inner city." In *Good Times*, 1. New York: Random House, 1969.

Clifton, Lucille. "my mama moved among the days." In *Good Times*, 2. New York: Random House, 1969.

Coffee, Robin. "Blood of a Warrior." *A Scar upon Our Voice*, 76. Albuquerque: University of New Mexico Press, 2005.

Coffee, Robin. "In from the Cold." *A Scar upon Our Voice*, 14. Albuquerque: University of New Mexico Press, 2005.

Coffee, Robin. "No Other Way." *A Scar upon Our Voice*, 22. Albuquerque: University of New Mexico Press, 2005.

Coffee, Robin. "Voices in the Water." *A Scar upon Our Voice*, 7. Albuquerque: University of New Mexico Press, 2005.

Coffee, Robin. "Warriors of This Time." *A Scar upon Our Voice*, 70. Albuquerque: University of New Mexico Press, 2005.

Corey, Frederick C., and Catherine T. Motoyama. "Toward Cultural Awareness through the Performance of Literary Texts." *MELUS* 16, no. 4 (1989): 75–86.

Cornell, Stephan. "The New Indian Politics." In *American Indians and U.S. Politics*. Edited by John M. Meyer. Westport, CT: Praeger Publishers, 2002.

Cox, Gary. *Existentialism and Excess: The Life and Times of Jean-Paul Sartre.* New York: Bloomsbury Academic, 2016.

"Coyote Hills Regional Park." *East Bay Regional Park District*. Accessed September 3, 2019.

Craps, Stef. "Beyond Eurocentrism: Trauma Theory in the Global Age." In *The Future of Trauma Theory: Contemporary Literary and Cultural Criticism*, edited by Gert Buelens, Sam Durrant, and Robert Eaglestone. New York: Routledge, 2014.

Craps, Stef. *Postcolonial Witnessing: Trauma Out of Bounds.* New York: Palgrave McMillan, 2015.

Culbertson, Roberta. "Embodied Memory, Transcendence, and Telling: Recounting Trauma, Re-Establishing the Self Author(s)." *New Literary History* 26.1 (1995): 169–95.

Cunningham, Scarlett. "The Limits of Celebration in Lucille Clifton's Poetry: Writing the Aging Woman's Body." *Frontiers: A Journal of Women Studies* 35, no. 2 (2014): 30–58.

Daniels, Roger. *Prisoners without Trial: Japanese Americans in World War II.* New York: Hill, 1993.

Derricotte, Toi. "Won't You Celebrate with Me: Remembering Lucille Clifton." *Callaloo* 33, no. 2 (2010): 373–79.

Dragulescu, Luminita M. "The Middle Passage and Race-Based Trauma." In *Trauma and Literature*, edited by J. Roger Kurtz. Cambridge: Cambridge University Press, 2018.

Drucker, Alison R. "The Influence of Western Women on the Anti-Footbinding Movement 1840–1911." *Historical Reflections/Réflexions Historiques* 8, no. 3 (1981): 179–99.

Eyerman, Ron. *Cultural Trauma: Slavery and the Formation of African American Identity.* Cambridge: Cambridge University Press, 2001.

Fuchs, Anne. *A Space of Anxiety: Dislocation and Abjection in Modern German-Jewish Literature.* Atlanta: Rodopi, 1999.

Fuller, Hoyt W. "Towards a Black Aesthetic." In *Within the Circle: An Anthology of African American Literary Criticism from the Harlem Renaissance to the Present*, edited by Angelyn Michell, 199–206. Durham, NC: Duke University Press, 1994.

Gal, Susan. "Language and Political Economy." *Annual Review of Anthropology* 18 (1989): 358.

Garloff, Hatja. *Words from Abroad: Trauma and Displacement in Postwar German Jewish Writer.* Detroit: Wayne State University Press, 2005.

Gower, Calvin W. "The CCC Indian Division: Aid for Depressed Americans, 1933–1942." *Minnesota History* 43, no. 1 (1972): 3–13.

Grisham, Kathleen. "20th Century Art: Neo-Plasticism." Instructor Homepage. *West Valley College.* Accessed October 25, 2018.

Grotjohn, Robert. "Remapping Internment: A Postcolonial Reading of Mitsuye Yamada, Lawson Fusao Inada, and Janice Mirikitani." *Western American Literature* 38, no. 3 (2003): 246–70.

Harding, Rachel E. "Authority, History, and Everyday Mysticism in the Poetry of Lucille Clifton: A Womanist View." *Meridians: Feminism, Race, Transnationalism* 12, no. 1 (2014): 36–57.

Harjani, Emilia Tetty. "The Feminist Voice in Lucille Clifton's 'The Thirty Eighth Year,' 'Miss Rosie' and 'Final Note to Clark.'" *Litera* 12, no. 1 (2013).

Harris, William J. "Introduction." *The LeRoi Jones /Amiri Baraka Reader*, edited by William J. Harris, xvii–xxx. New York: Thumermouth, 1991.

Harrison, Summer. "'We Need New Stories': Trauma, Storytelling, and the Mapping of Environmental Injustice in Linda Hogan's *Solar Storms* and Standing Rock." *American Indian Quarterly* 43, no. 1 (2019): 1–35.

Hartman, Saidiya V. *Scenes of Subjection: Terror, Slavery, and Self-Making in Nineteenth-Century America.* New York: Oxford University Press, 1997.

Hogan, Linda. "Cities behind Glass." In *Seeing through the Sun*, 59. Amherst: University of Massachusetts Press, 1985.

Hogan, Linda. "The Truth Is." In *Seeing through the Sun*, 4–5. Amherst: University of Massachusetts Press, 1985.

Inada, Lawson Fusao. "Healing Gila." In *Drawing the Line*, 110–11. Minneapolis: Coffee House, 1997.

Inada, Lawson Fusao. "Legends from Camp." In *Legends from Camp*, 7–25. Minneapolis: Coffee House, 1993.

"Indian Health Disparities." *Indian Health Service.* United States Department of Health and Human Services. Accessed October 19, 2018.

Irwin, Lee. "Freedom, Law, and Prophecy: A Brief History of Native American Religious Resistance." In *American Indians and U.S. Politics*, edited by John M. Meyer, 75–90. Westport, CT: Praeger Publishers, 2002.

Jaskoski, Helen, and Mitsuye Yamada. "A *MELUS* Interview: Mitsuye Yamada." *MELUS* 15, no. 1 (1988): 97–108.

Jerg-Bretzke, Lucia, Steffen Walter, Kerstin Limbrecht-Ecklundt, and Harald C. Traue. "Emotional Ambivalence and Post-Traumatic Stress Disorder (PTSD) in Soldiers during Military Operations." *Psycho-social Medicine* 10 (2013): Doc03.

Johnson, Troy. "The Occupation of Alcatraz Island: Roots of American Indian Activism." *Wicazo Sa Review* 10, no. 2 (1994): 76.

Johnson, Troy. "We Hold the Rock: The Alcatraz Indian Occupation." *National Park Service*. United States Department of the Interior. Accessed October 28, 2018.

Jones, LeRoi. *Black Music*. London: Macgibbo & Kee, 1969.

Jones, LeRoi. *Blues People: Negro Music in White America*. Santa Barbara: Praeger, 1980.

Jones, LeRoi. "The Myth of a 'Negro Literature.'" In *Within the Circle: An Anthology of African American Literary Criticism from the Harlem Renaissance to the Present*, edited by Angelyn Mitchell, 165–71. Durham, NC: Duke University Press, 1994.

"kachina." In *Britannica Concise Encyclopedia*, by Encyclopaedia Britannica. Britannica Digital Learning, 2017.

"kachina." In *Chambers Dictionary of the Unexplained*, edited by Una McGovern. Chambers Harrap, 2007.

Kalaidjian, Walter. *The Edge of Modernism: American Poetry and the Traumatic Past*. Baltimore: Johns Hopkins University Press, 2006.

Kaplan, Ann E. *Trauma Culture*. Piscataway: Rutgers University Press, 2005.

Knight, Etheridge. "Bones of My Father." In *The Essential Etheridge Knight*, 40. Pittsburgh: University of Pittsburgh Press, 1986.

Knight, Etheridge. "Once on a Night in the Delta: A Report from Hell." In *The Essential Etheridge Knight*. Pittsburgh: University of Pittsburgh Press, 1986.

Komunyakaa, Yusef. "Annabelle." In *Copacetic*, 8. Middletown: Wesleyan University Press, 1984.

Komunyakaa, Yusef. "Family Tree." In *Copacetic*, 96–99. Middletown: Wesleyan University Press, 1984.

Komunyakaa, Yusef. "Reflections." In *Copacetic*, 7. Middletown: Wesleyan University Press, 1984.

Kostova, Bilyana Vanyova. "'Time to Write Them Off'? Impossible Voices and the Problem of Representing Trauma in *The Virgin Suicides*." In *Trauma and Literature*, edited by J. Roger Kurtz. Cambridge: Cambridge University Press, 2018.

Kristeva, Julia. *Powers of Horror: An Essay on Abjection*. New York: Columbia University Press, 1982.

Kunce, Catherine. "Feasting on Famine in Linda Hogan's *Solar Storms*." *Studies in American Indian Literatures* 21, no. 2 (2009): 50–70.

May, Philip A. "Overview of Alcohol Abuse Epidemiology for American Indian Populations." National Center for Biotechnological Information. Accessed November 16, 2018.

McAdams, Janet. "'Ways in the World': Formal Poetics in Linda Hogan's *Rounding the Human Corners.*" *The Kenyon Review* 32, no. 1 (2010): 226–35.

Mehrvand, Ahad. "A Postcolonial Reading of Amiri Baraka's 21st Century Political Poem on America." *International Journal of Education and Literacy Studies* 4, no. 4 (2016): 21–29.

Moten, Fred. *In the Break: The Aesthetics of the Black Radical Tradition.* Minneapolis: University of Minnesota Press, 2003.

Neal, Larry. "The Black Arts Movement." In *Within the Circle: An Anthology of African American Literary Criticism from the Harlem Renaissance to the Present*, edited by Angelyn Mitchell, 184–98. Durham: Duke University Press, 1994.

Okihiro, Gary. *Margins and Mainstream: Asians in American History and Culture.* Seattle: University of Washington Press, 1994.

Patterson, Anita Haya. "Resistance to Images of the Internment: Mitsuye Yamada's *Camp Notes.*" *MELUS* 23, no. 3 (1998): 103–27.

Plath, Sylvia. "Daddy." In *Poetry Foundation.* Accessed September 27, 2018.

Robben, Antonius C. G. M., and Marcelo M. Suarez-Orozco. "Management of Collective Trauma." In *Cultures under Siege: Collective Violence and Trauma*, edited by Marcelo M. Suarez Orozco and Antonius C. G. M. Robben, 43–47. Cambridge: Cambridge University Press, 2000.

Roney, Patrick. "The Paradox of Experience: Black Art and Black Idiom in the Work of Amiri Baraka." *African American Review* 37, no. 2/3 (2003): 407–21.

Roxworthy, Emily. *The Spectacle of Japanese American Trauma: Racial Performativity and World War II.* Honolulu: University of Hawaii Press, 2008.

Schultz, Kathy Lou. "Amiri Baraka's *Wise Why's Y's*: Lineages of the Afro-Modernist Epic." *JML: Journal of Modern Literature* 35, no. 3 (2012): 25–50.

Soga, Keiho. "A fellow prisoner." In *Poets behind Barbed Wire*, edited and translated by Jiro Nakano and Kay Nakano, 57. Honolulu: Bamboo Ridge, 1983.

Soga, Keiho. "Like a dog." In *Poets behind Barbed Wire*, edited and translated by Jiro Nakano and Kay Nakano, 19. Honolulu: Bamboo Ridge, 1983.

Soga, Keiho. "There is nothing." In *Poets behind Barbed Wire*, edited and translated by Jiro Nakano and Kay Nakano, 21. Honolulu: Bamboo Ridge, 1983.

Sommers, Ephraim Scott. "The Poem of Anger: Amiri Baraka, Tory Dent, and Adrian C. Louis." *Cream City Review* 40, no. 2 (2016): 40–63.

St. Onge, Jeffrey, and Jennifer Moore. "Poetry as a Form of Dissent: John F. Kennedy, Amiri Baraka, and the Politics of Art in Rhetorical Democracy." *Rhetoric Review* 35, no. 4 (2016): 335–47.

Steele, Cassie Premo. *We Heal from Memory: Sexton, Lorde, Anzaldúa, and the Poetry of Witness.* New York: Palgrave, 2000.

Stringer, Dorothy. *Not Even Past: Race, Historical Trauma, and Subjectivity in Faulkner, Larsen, and Van Vechten.* New York: Fordham University Press, 2010.

"Tanka: Poetic Form." *Academy of American Poets.* Accessed June 13, 2019.

Vernon, Irene S. "'We Were Those Who Walked out of Bullets and Hunger': Representation of Trauma and Healing in *Solar Storms.*" *American Indian Quarterly* 36, no. 1 (2012): 34–49.

Visser, Irene. "Trauma and Power in Postcolonial Literary Studies." In *Contemporary Approaches in Literary Trauma Theory*, edited by Michelle Balaev. New York: Palgrave McMillan, 2014.

Yamada, Mitsuye. "Cincinnati." In *Camp Notes and Other Poems*, 32–33. Berkeley: Shameless Hussy, 1976.

Yamada, Mitsuye. "The Question of Loyalty." In *Camp Notes and Other Poems*, 29. Berkeley: Shameless Hussy, 1976.

Zinn, Howard. *A People's History of the United States*. New York: Harper Collins, 2005.

Index

abjection, 4–5, 9, 22–24, 27–28, 31, 33, 36, 38–40, 43–44, 46–47, 49, 54, 55, 57–61, 72, 77, 87–88, 90–91, 94–96, 99, 105–110, 115, 134–35, 137–39
Alcatraz, 103, 104, 107, 116–19, 122, 129
ambivalence, 2–5, 9, 20, 36, 38, 44, 46, 48, 50, 59–60, 72, 77–79, 84, 90–93, 95–96, 106, 110–12, 114–16, 118, 121, 125–26, 128–29, 133–35, 137, 139–140
Auerhahn, Nanette and Dori Laub, 12–14, 15, 17–18, 27, 59

Baraka, Amiri: "Black Dada Nihilismus," 75–84; "Legacy," 75–76, 87–91; "Reggae or Not," 85
Bleger, Jose, 2
Blue Cloud, Peter: "Alcatraz," 116, 118–22; "For Ace," 122–28
Brave Heart, Maria Yellow Horse, 6, 7–8, 72, 104–5
Brooks, Cleanth, 2
Burt, Ryan, 55–56

Clifton, Lucille: "if something should happen," 96–100; "in the inner city," 92–94; "my mama moved among the days," 94–96

Coffee, Robin: "Blood of a Warrior," 111–14; "Voices in the Water," 107–111, 115
collective trauma, 6, 21, 42
community, vii, 1, 6–7, 9–11, 19–20, 26–28, 31–32, 65, 69, 71–72, 75–76, 81, 89, 91, 104, 107–8, 115, 123, 127–28, 143–44
coping, 8–10, 13, 18–19, 22, 26–28, 33, 81, 87, 105, 138
Corey, Frederick C. and Catherine T. Motoyama, 44
Cornell, Stephan, 118
Craps, Stef: "Beyond Eurocentrism: Trauma Theory in the Global Age," 33; *Postcolonial Witnessing: Trauma Out of Bounds*, 4
Culbertson, Roberta, 27
Cunningham, Scarlett, 92

Daniels, Roger, 34, 39, 58, 62
Derricotte, Toi, 92
distress, 14, 19–20, 28, 31, 35, 37, 42, 47, 56, 83, 85–86, 92, 100, 103, 105, 132, 136
Dragulescu, Luminita M., 4, 11

empowerment, 1, 5, 11, 19–20, 24, 27–28, 31, 33–34, 65–66, 69, 75,

95–97, 100, 103–5, 107, 110, 112, 115, 129
Eyerman, Ron, 4, 70–71, 72

fragmented/fragmentation, 10, 14, 16, 21–22, 24, 89–91, 96, 110, 138
Fuchs, Anne, 22–23, 38, 90, 94, 138
Fuller, Hoyt W., 71

Gal, Susan, 24
Gower, Calvin W., 131–32
Grotjohn, Robert, 56

Harding, Rachel E., 92
Harjani, Emilia Tetty, 92
Harrison, Summer, 129
Harris, William J., 75, 87
Hartman, Saidiya V., 85
historical trauma, ii, vii, 4–11, 17–21, 24–26, 31–32, 40, 42–44, 55, 64–65, 69, 72, 74–77, 79, 83, 86–87, 90–92, 96–97, 99–100, 103–5, 107, 109–10, 115, 120–21, 126–27, 129, 132, 134, 136, 143–44
Hogan, Linda: "Cities behind Glass," 135–40; "The Truth Is," 129–34

identity, 4, 21–24, 36, 38, 47–49, 53, 57–59, 61, 63, 70–71, 74, 76, 78, 80, 89, 109, 118–20, 129–37, 139
Inada, Lawson Fusao: "Healing Gila," 61–66; "Legends from Camp," 56–60
Irwin, Lee, 117
isolation, 3, 23, 27, 33, 36–40, 43, 49, 54, 59–60, 72, 91–92, 96, 99–100, 105–9, 116, 119, 121, 127, 129, 138

Jaskoski, Helen and Mitsuye Yamada, 54
Jerg–Bretzke, Lucia, Steffen Walter, Kerstin Limbrecht–Ecklundt, and Harald C
Traue, 3–4

Johnson, Troy: "The Occupation of Alcatraz Island: Roots of American Indian Activism," 117–18; "We Hold the Rock: The Alcatraz Indian Occupation," 116
Jones, LeRoi, 71–72

kachina, 119–120
Kalaidjian, Walter, 9, 12
Kaplan, Ann E., 6
Knight, Etheridge: "Bones of My Father," 22; "Once on a Night in the Delta: A Report from Hell," 18–19
Komunyakaa, Yusef: "Annabelle," 15; "Family Tree," 15; "Reflection," 15
Kostova, Bilyana Vanyova, 11
Kristeva, Julia, 4, 22, 38
Kunce, Catherine, 129

McAdams, Janet, 129
Mehrvand, Ahad, 76
Moten, Fred, 73, 79, 85–86

Neal, Larry, 70, 71, 74

Okihiro, Gary, 32

Patterson, Anita Haya, 44, 53
Plath, Sylvia, 18, 60
post-traumatic stress disorder (PTSD), ii, ix, 3–4, 8, 21, 72, 104–5

racism, ix, 11, 32, 34, 38, 49, 51, 54, 65, 74, 86–87, 91, 97, 105, 111, 126, 128, 143–44
Robben, Antonius C. G. M., and Marcelo M. Suarez–Orozco, 7
Roney, Patrick, 78
Roxworthy, Emily, 33

Schultz, Kathy Lou, 75
Soga, Keiho: "A fellow prisoner," 41–43; "Like a dog," 38–40; "There is nothing," 36–38

Sommers, Ephraim Scott, 76
St. Onge, Jeffrey and Jennifer Moore, 75–76
Steele, Cassie Premo, 1, 9–10, 12, 16, 27
Stringer, Dorothy, 20

tanka, 35–37
trauma, ii, viii, 1, 3–28, 31–36, 38, 40–44, 47, 49–50, 52–57, 59–65, 69–70, 72–92, 94–97, 99–100, 103–7, 110–16, 118–23, 125–36, 138–40, 143–44
trauma as metaphor/traumatic metaphor, 14, 17–18, 59, 73, 111, 116, 123, 128
traumatic figurative language, 16–19, 27, 31, 33, 36, 39–44, 49, 59–61, 65, 69, 72–73, 80, 82, 91, 97, 99, 106, 110, 112, 115–16, 119, 122, 124–25, 127–30, 133–34, 140
traumatic memory, 9, 12–13, 16–17, 20, 26, 43, 55

unhomeliness, 22–24, 27, 31, 33, 36, 40, 43, 46–47, 54, 59–60, 72, 87, 90–94, 99, 105–7, 109–10, 115, 117, 129, 134–35, 137–40
unresolved grief, 8, 104, 106, 113, 128

Vernon, Irene S.: "'We Were Those Who Walked out of Bullets and Hunger': Representation of Trauma ; and Healing in *Solar Storms*," 129
Visser, Irene: "Trauma and Power in Postcolonial Literary Studies," 5

Yamada, Mitsuye: "Cincinnati," 49–55; "The Question of Loyalty," 44–49

Zinn, Howard, 112

About the Author

Jamie D. Barker, PhD, is a senior lecturer at Texas Woman's University in Denton, Texas, where he teaches poetry, minority literature, and advanced grammar and composition. Dr. Barker has had articles published in such places as *The Explicator* and wrote the Foreword to *Education in a Post-factual World*. Additionally, Dr. Barker worked as an editorial assistant for *Anxiety, Stress, and Coping*. Beyond his scholarship, editorial work, and teaching, Dr. Barker is also an internationally published and award-winning poet. Currently, he is working on a book-length examination of several of August Wilson's plays.

www.ingramcontent.com/pod-product-compliance
Lightning Source LLC
Chambersburg PA
CBHW050909300426
44111CB00010B/1442